CHRIST CONSCIOUSNESS
The True Way
Breaking Free from Fear and Embracing the Power of Divine Love

Revised Edition 1.1 – June 2025

Akashic Knowledge Publishing

Copyright © 2025 John Lawrence

The right of John Lawrence to be identified as the Author of the Work has been asserted by him in accordance with the Copyright, Designs and Patents Act 1988.

First published in 2025
by AKASHIC KNOWLEDGE PUBLISHING

All rights reserved. No part of this publication may be reproduced, stored in a retrieval system, or transmitted, in any form or by any means, without the prior written permission of the publisher, nor be otherwise circulated in any form of binding or cover other than that in which it is published and without a similar condition being imposed on the subsequent purchaser.

ISBN: 979-8-9925572-0-6 (Digital Online)
ISBN: 979-8-9925572-1-3 (Paperback)

This is Edition 1.1, revised and expanded June 2025.

AKASHIC KNOWLEDGE PUBLISHING
30 Walnut Ln
Deatsville, AL 36022
United States

https://akashicknowledge.com/

Editor's Note on the Revised Edition (1.1)

Since the original publication of *Christ Consciousness – The True Way* on February 22, 2025, new insights have continued to emerge, both through spiritual revelation and deeper historical study. This revised edition reflects those discoveries, integrating expanded context around Yeshua's protest in the Temple, the symbolic role of Mary Magdalene, the deeper meaning behind Da Vinci's *Last Supper*, and a clearer understanding of the ego as the archetypal "Beast" of Revelation.

Each of these additions strengthens the message at the heart of this work: that Christ did not come to found a religion of fear, but to awaken Love through direct communion with the Divine. May this revised edition offer an even greater invitation to live in the liberating frequency of Christ Consciousness.

For those following the broader arc of this exploration, this book is the first in a trilogy. The upcoming volumes: **Human Consciousness – Cycles Through Time** and **Universal Consciousness – The Quantum Key** will continue to expand the story of our spiritual evolution across time and space.

Table of Contents

Introduction	1
Chapter-1: Rediscovering Jesus Beyond Dogma	**3**
Balance From Polarity	3
The Dance of Duality: Balance in a Polarized World	4
The Morning Star: Christ and Lucifer = Duality	5
Unity in Opposites: The Key to Balance	6
Heart-Brain Coherence	8
The Truth About Jesus	11
The Historicity of Jesus	12
Conclusion	17
Chapter-2: The Suppression of Knowledge	**18**
The Truth About the Bible	18
The History of the Bible	19
Rome and the Council of Nicaea	20
Biblical Edits	23
The Historicity of the Bible	26
Issues with the Old Testament	30
Deuteronomy	31
The Left-Brain of Deuteronomy	36
The Omnipotence of God	40
Conclusion	41
Chapter-3: Other Ancient Texts	**42**
The Epic of Gilgamesh	42
The Eridu Genesis Story	43
Chapter-4: The Concept of Hell	**46**
Gehenna	46
Jesus on Hell	47
Concept of Eternal Torment	51
Chapter-5: Gnosticism	**52**
The Essenes - Jesus and John the Baptist	55
The End of Sacrifice: A Final Act of Mercy	58
The Ebionites: Guardians of the Original Teachings	60
Paul's Struggles Against the Original Disciples	66

The Spouter of Lies and Paul's Gospel	68
Paul's Troubles in Ephesus	79
Revelation's Theology: Aligning with Christ, Not Paul	81
The Roman Catholic Suppression of Ebionite Teachings	84
The Cathars vs. The Empire	85
Chapter-6: Others Similar to Jesus	**88**
Krishna - Circa 3228–3102 BC	88
Zoroaster - Circa 1500–1000 BC	91
Buddha - Circa 563–483 BC	93
The Law of One - 1981-1984	96
The Law of One Prayer of Christ	99
Chapter-7: Reincarnation	**101**
The Many Lives of Christ	105
The Law of One: Cayce's Insights	108
The Great Pyramid as a Tool for Ascension	109
Thoth and the Wisdom of the Law of One	110
Hermes Trismegistus and the Great Pyramid	110
Chapter-8: Christ Consciousness: The Christ in You	**112**
From Sin Consciousness to Christ Consciousness	114
The Hermetic Synthesis	117
Christ Consciousness and the True Identity of Jesus	119
The Sacred Message in Da Vinci's Last Supper	121
The Holy Trinity	123
The Trinity of Consciousness	127
The Ego, the Beast, and the Death of Separation	131
The Gospel of Paul: A Message Tainted by Ego	132
The Return to Oneness	133
Chapter-9: The Power of Prayer	**135**
A Personal Experience	136
The Lord's Prayer	140
Chapter-10: The Importance of Meditation	**145**
Chapter-11: Re-Examine the Words of Christ	**153**
Final Words	156
Bibliography	**157**

Introduction

We live in a world caught in the throes of conflict with values clashing, ideologies colliding, and truths buried beneath centuries of dogma. Yet, if you strip away the superficial differences, you'll find a surprising revelation: most religions and philosophies actually tell the same story. Light versus darkness. Good versus evil. The cosmic dance of duality. Peel back the layers, and a universal truth begins to emerge that transcends cultural boundaries and doctrines.

But amidst these ancient truths lies a new "religion" that claims no temples, yet dominates every corner of modern life: **Materialism.** With its relentless focus on the tangible, the measurable, and the physical, Materialism is the true one-world religion of our time. Like any faith, it rests on assumptions…assumptions that quantum mechanics is now beginning to unravel. And while this will be explored in a subsequent book, let me offer a hint: the latest breakthroughs in quantum physics validate concepts that ancient Eastern philosophies have understood for thousands of years. Materialism is not the eternal truth it pretends to be.

But that is not today's focus. Today, we turn to the largest religion in the world, with a staggering 2.4 billion followers: **Christianity.** How did the teachings of a humble carpenter from Galilee grow into the world's greatest religious movement? Was it the undeniable truth of his message, or was there something else at play that was hidden, manipulated, and engineered to serve an agenda?

As the son of a Methodist minister, I grew up steeped in the teachings of Christ. I've stood on stages as a worship leader, proclaiming the faith to congregations. But even for me, doubts crept in. Cracks began to appear in the foundation of everything I had believed. I couldn't ignore the inconsistencies, the questions no one seemed willing to answer. So, I began a quest, not just for faith, but for **Truth.** What I discovered shook me to my core.

This book is the result of that journey. It's a challenge to everything you think you know about Jesus, the Church, and the faith you may hold dear. Are you ready to pull back the curtain and confront the untold story behind the world's most powerful religion? If so, let us begin…

Chapter-1: Rediscovering Jesus Beyond Dogma

Balance From Polarity

In the year 1998 I was given a very simple concept which turned out to be one of the most profound things I have ever been taught. In this life, **Balance is the Key to Everything**! At the time I was in my second year of martial arts training, so naturally this was one area in my life where I found this statement to be very much true on a physical level. However, this was ironically only a very simple example of the innate truth of that statement. I soon learned that this simple concept actually does hold true in all facets of life. I realized that too much of anything, ultimately has a negative impact on your life. Excessive indulgence in anything, whether food, material wealth, or even water, can ultimately harm your well-being. One can imagine anything on the physical plane and you will inevitably come to the understanding that too much of a good thing can be bad for you.

The same holds true on a spiritual or energetic level as well. If you lean too far to one side or the other, then you will eventually come to learn that it has a negative impact on your life. Many of the ascended masters throughout history have taught this principle through their teachings, as well as their mystical associations. The names Quetzacoatl and Kukulkan, of the meso-american tradition, both mean "Feathered Serpent". This name implies the duality of extremes, where the vulture or eagle flies higher than any other animal, and the serpent or snake crawls on the ground lower than any other. The name of Incan god Viracocha means "Foam of the Sea". Where does the foam of the sea reside but on the shoreline balanced between the land and the sea. Even Christ was called the "Morning Star", alluding to the planet Venus, which is the Morning Star for 263 days, and the Evening Star for 263 days. Thus evoking the concept of balance in duality.

Therefore, I contend that this is truly one of the most prophetically simplistic concepts that one can grasp in their journey through life. If you can implement this simple principle that balance is the key to everything, then you will have a much more peaceful life. However, while the principle of balance offers a pathway to harmony, the reality we face often feels far from balanced. Instead, we find ourselves immersed in a world deeply rooted in polarity, where opposites seem to define every aspect of existence. To fully grasp the importance of balance, we must first understand the pervasive role that duality plays in shaping our perceptions, choices, and experiences.

The Dance of Duality: Balance in a Polarized World

The irony of the above concepts about balance is that we currently live in a world that appears to be anything but balanced. In stark contrast, we actually live in a time that is dominated by polarity on all sides. We all seem to see things from the standpoint of Good versus Evil, Right versus Wrong, or Light versus Darkness. There is a deeper purpose behind the concept of diametric opposition. For how can one fully appreciate the nature of good without first understanding the experience of bad? How can the rewards of righteousness be recognized without encountering the challenges of wrongdoing? Or, how can one fully appreciate the Light, unless he has first been fully immersed in total Darkness?

The concept of polarity completely saturates this realm. Whether it is in politics, religion, gender, or even our beloved sporting events. Everywhere one looks there is polarity staring right back at you in the face. It seems to be directly baked into reality itself when one contemplates the examples of polarity that are part of our everyday lives. Even life springs forth out of the necessity for the union of polarity. For when male joins with female, which both represent the polarity of gender, a new life is conceived. Yet, even this new life is an example of the split from Unity to Polarity from the very beginning, as the first cell splits into two. Thus, polarity is something that we simply cannot avoid in this life…

This interplay of opposites is not merely a human construct but a cosmic principle embedded in spiritual and mythological narratives across cultures. Among the most profound symbols of duality is the Morning Star, a title that intriguingly connects both Christ and Lucifer, illustrating the paradoxical dance between light and shadow within our shared spiritual journey.

The Morning Star: Christ and Lucifer = Duality

The title of the Morning Star is one of the most intriguing dualities in spiritual symbolism, attributed to both Christ and Lucifer in various religious texts. At first glance, this may seem contradictory. For how can the same title apply to figures seen as such polar opposites? Yet, this shared designation reveals a deeper esoteric truth about the nature of duality in our plane of existence.

In the Book of Revelation, Jesus declares, "*I am the Root and the Offspring of David, and the **bright Morning Star**"* (**Revelation 22:16**). This title signifies the light of divine truth, the herald of a new dawn, and the spiritual illumination that dispels darkness. It represents the pure, uncorrupted light that brings clarity and guidance, much like Venus appearing as the Morning Star before sunrise.

On the other hand, Lucifer, whose name literally means "light-bringer" or "bearer of light," was once seen as a powerful angel who embodied divine radiance before his fall.

Isaiah 14:12 (KJV): "*How art thou fallen from heaven, O Lucifer, **son of the morning**! how art thou cut down to the ground, which didst weaken the nations!*"

In this verse, Lucifer is described as the **"son of the morning"**, which is a poetic reference to the Morning Star (Venus). The association with the Morning Star reflects Lucifer's original role as a bringer of enlightenment and knowledge. His rebellion and subsequent fall from grace symbolize the descent into shadow, the separation from the divine source, and the dual nature of seeking knowledge without wisdom. This is the true nature of the world's current religion of Materialism.

This shared symbolism points to a cosmic duality inherent in the human experience, which is the interplay between light and shadow, unity and separation, spiritual ascent and material descent. The Morning Star symbolizes both the promise of spiritual enlightenment, as embodied by Christ, and the allure of self-centered knowledge, as represented by Lucifer.

In esoteric traditions, the Morning Star is linked to the planet Venus, which appears both as the Morning Star and the Evening Star. This dual appearance mirrors the dual aspects of Christ and Lucifer, with one heralding the dawn of spiritual light and the other symbolizing the fall into the night of materialism and separation. It reflects the ancient Hermetic principle of "As above, so below," where the celestial dance of Venus becomes a metaphor for the dual forces at play within each of us. Ultimately, this shared title invites us to look beyond the simplistic binary of good and evil, and to recognize the deeper unity of opposites. It calls us to integrate the light and the shadow within ourselves, transcending duality and embracing the path of spiritual wholeness.

Unity in Opposites: The Key to Balance

The left side of the brain predominantly governs logical thinking, analysis, language, and linear reasoning. It's focused on details, sequential tasks, and interpreting the physical world around us. Due to these characteristics, it is often linked with a more traditionally 'masculine' energy. In contrast, the right hemisphere is connected to creativity, intuition, holistic perception, and non-verbal comprehension. It tends to engage with spiritual insights, a sense of unity, and deeper, mystical experiences, aligning it with what is commonly seen as 'feminine' energy.[1]

In our modern Western culture, there is a strong dominance of left-brain thinking. I believe this phase was a necessary part of human evolution, helping us deepen our understanding of the material world and develop technologies that support our long-term goals as a species. However, this heavy focus on logical, linear, and materialistic thinking has come at a cost. It has suppressed many qualities linked to

---

[1] Jill Bolte Taylor, *My Stroke of Insight: A Brain Scientist's Personal Journey* (New York: Viking, 2008), 58-63.

the right hemisphere, such as intuition, energetic perception, and the ability to access deeper spiritual truths. This imbalance has distanced us from the profound spiritual wisdom of ancient cultures, which often maintained a more holistic approach to knowledge.

In many ancient cultures, knowledge and consciousness were approached in a more balanced manner, where both the rational left-brain processes and the intuitive right-brain processes were equally valued[2]. Ancient shamans, mystics, and spiritual leaders often entered altered states of consciousness to access the non-linear, non-verbal wisdom associated with the right brain. This practice allowed them to connect with universal consciousness and gain a deeper understanding of existence. In these societies, the left-brain abilities such as organization, architecture, mathematics, and technology were not seen as separate from the right-brain qualities of spiritual insight and mystical experience. Instead, these aspects were harmonized to provide a more complete perspective on reality. This integration is evident in the architecture, art, and religious practices of many ancient civilizations.

Over time, particularly with the rise of materialism and institutionalized religion, the intuitive and mystical insights of the right brain were increasingly overshadowed. As society became more focused on left-brain thinking, which emphasizes logic, linear progression, and empirical evidence, the deep, intuitive wisdom that once formed the core of human understanding was dismissed or regarded as superstitious and irrational. This ancient shamanic and mystical knowledge appears to have been deliberately suppressed, as it posed a challenge to the control structures that relied on a materialistic, left-brain-dominated worldview.[3]

There is a growing movement of people advocating for a reconnection with right-brain modes of consciousness as a means to heal the modern soul and reclaim lost wisdom. This reconnection is seen not only as a personal spiritual journey, but also as a crucial step for the

---

[2] Joseph Campbell, *The Power of Myth* (New York: Doubleday, 1988), 122-126.

[3] Michael Harner, *The Way of the Shaman* (San Francisco: Harper & Row, 1980), 45-50.

survival of humanity. Without a harmonious balance, society risks continuing on a trajectory of environmental degradation, existential crises, spiritual disconnection, and, ultimately, self-destruction[4]. By integrating the strengths of both brain hemispheres, we can renew our relationship with the Earth, with one another, and with the broader cosmic order. Later in this book, we will delve deeper into the adverse effects that an overly left-brain-focused philosophy has had on our culture.

I believe the future of humanity depends on rediscovering this balance between the hemispheres. Modern science, particularly quantum physics, is beginning to uncover truths that mirror ancient wisdom, such as the non-locality of consciousness and the interconnectedness of all things. This could mark the beginning of a new era of integration, where left-brain logic and right-brain intuition come together to offer a more complete picture of reality. For Jesus said in the Gospel of Thomas, "**When you make the two into one**, *you will become children of Adam, and when you say, 'Mountain, move from here!' it will move.*"

Achieving unity between opposites requires more than a mental understanding of balance; it involves aligning the deeper connections within ourselves. Beyond the interplay of our brain hemispheres lies another profound harmony, that between the heart and the brain. Exploring this relationship reveals how coherence between these vital centers can unlock new dimensions of emotional and spiritual well-being.

Heart-Brain Coherence

Common sayings like "think with your heart" or "let your heart guide you" suggest a deeper truth worth exploring. These phrases may carry deeper truths than they appear to at first glance. The heart is far more than just a mechanical pump[5]; it is an intelligent organ with its own intricate nervous system, often referred to as the "heart-brain" or "heart

---

[4] Graham Hancock, *Heaven's Mirror: Quest for the Lost Civilization* (London: Michael Joseph, 1998), 150-155.
[5] Rollin McCraty, *Science of the Heart: Exploring the Role of the Heart in Human Performance* (Boulder Creek, CA: HeartMath Institute, 2015), 22-25.

intelligence." The heart contains a network of neurons similar to those in the brain, allowing it to operate somewhat independently. It sends signals that influence our thoughts, emotions, and responses, highlighting the powerful connection between the heart and our overall well-being.

In a remarkable case documented by neuropsychologist Paul Pearsall, an 8-year-old girl received a heart transplant from a 10-year-old girl who had been murdered[6]. Following the transplant, the recipient began having recurring nightmares, vividly detailing the events of the murder. The descriptions were so accurate that they ultimately helped identify the murderer and solve the case. This incident supports theories suggesting that the heart, with its own intrinsic nervous system, may store memories independently of the brain. Such examples challenge our traditional understanding of memory storage and highlight the deeper connection between the heart and brain.

The concept of "coherence" refers to a state where different components of a system operate smoothly and harmoniously, resulting in a unified and clear experience. Heart-brain coherence explores the interaction between the heart and brain, revealing how they influence our physical, emotional, and spiritual well-being. Research, especially from the HeartMath Institute, has shown that when the heart's rhythms synchronize with brain activity, it can create a state of enhanced mental clarity, emotional stability, and a greater sense of balance.

The heart generates the most powerful electromagnetic field of any organ in the human body, with an impressive range. Sensitive magnetometers have detected this field extending 3 to 4 feet beyond the body in every direction. Unlike the brain's electromagnetic field, the heart's field is significantly stronger and continuously interacts with our surroundings. Research from the HeartMath Institute[7], which focuses on heart-brain coherence and the heart's role in emotional and physiological processes, shows that the heart's electromagnetic field

---

[6] Paul Pearsall, *The Heart's Code: Tapping the Wisdom and Power of Our Heart Energy* (New York: Broadway Books, 1998), 101-105.
[7] HeartMath Institute Research Staff, *Heart Intelligence: Connecting with the Intuitive Guidance of the Heart* (Boulder Creek, CA: Waterfront Press, 2016), 33-35.

varies according to emotional states. Emotions like gratitude and love generate a stable, coherent field, while fear and anger result in chaotic, erratic patterns.

The heart and brain are in constant communication through the vagus nerve and other pathways within the nervous system[8]. While traditional views held that the brain primarily controls the body and emotions, recent studies have demonstrated that the heart actually sends twice as many signals to the brain as the brain sends to the heart. This bidirectional communication plays a vital role in cognitive functions, including attention, memory, problem-solving, and emotional regulation. Heart-brain coherence is the term used to describe the synchronization between the heart's rhythms and brainwaves. When these systems achieve coherence, they work together in a harmonious, efficient manner that enhances overall physical and mental performance.

Many ancient cultures viewed the heart as the seat of the soul, connecting humanity to higher states of consciousness. Perhaps we as humans need to take a more balanced approach to how we use both hemispheres of our brain, and then match our balanced brain approach with a more balanced level of Heart-Brian coherence. If we did this, then there is no telling how much we would advance physiologically, as well as mentally and emotionally, over a very short period of time.

For as Christ said in the **Gospel of Thomas**: "*When you **make the two into one**, and when you make the inner like the outer and the outer like the inner, and the **upper like the lower**, and when you **make male and female into a single one**, so that the male will not be male nor the female be female, when you make eyes in place of an eye, a hand in place of a hand, a foot in place of a foot, an image in place of an image, then **you will enter [the kingdom]**.*"

As we consider the profound connections between the heart and mind, it becomes evident that this inner harmony reflects a larger spiritual truth. Few figures embody this unity more deeply than Jesus, whose

---

[8] Stephen W. Porges, *The Polyvagal Theory: Neurophysiological Foundations of Emotions, Attachment, Communication, and Self-Regulation* (New York: W.W. Norton & Company, 2011), 68-72.

teachings reveal the transformative power of love and coherence, both within ourselves and in our relationship with the Divine.

The Truth About Jesus

Readers may hold deep-rooted beliefs that have drawn them to Christ's teachings and inspired a life of faith. This book is not here to dismantle your faith, but to invite you to experience the fullest potential of Christ's message, which is a message rooted in love, freedom, and higher understanding.

Christ's teachings have been a guiding light for countless souls. Yet over time, these teachings have been filtered through different lenses, especially during the Roman Empire's adoption and structuring of Christianity. Through that lens, certain interpretations of Christ's message emphasized fear and judgment. Yet, as Christ Himself taught, "*Judge not, lest you be judged*," and "*love your enemies and pray for those who persecute you*". These are the foundations of his message, which is one that transcends the limitations of fear, and embraces the boundless love of God. With this in mind, let us discover the Truth about Jesus.

This chapter begins by addressing one of the most frequently misunderstood arguments about the identity of Jesus. That is the idea that "Jesus" actually means "Hail Zeus," and that Jesus wasn't even his real name. Well, the "Hail Zeus" notion is literal nonsense, yet technically the second part is a correct assumption, just not for the reasons that antagonists will declare. The idea that the name "Jesus" means "Hail Zeus" is a misconception that stems from a misunderstanding of the linguistic evolution of the name "Jesus", and its Greek and Hebrew roots.

The name "Jesus" is derived from the Hebrew name Yeshua, which is a shortened form of Yehoshua, meaning "Yahweh is salvation" or "God saves." When the Hebrew Scriptures were translated into Greek, the name Yeshua was rendered as Iēsous, because Greek does not have the same sounds as Hebrew. Greek does not have the "sh" sound, so it was replaced with "s," and the ending was changed to fit Greek grammar. From Greek, the name Iēsous was transliterated into Latin as Iesus. In English, over time, this became "Jesus." The "J" sound in English is a relatively modern development in the evolution of the language, replacing the "I" in many names, including "Iesus."

So, let us dispel the persistent myth that the name "Jesus" is derived from "Hail Zeus." This misconception is unfounded and simply detracts from more meaningful discussions.

The Historicity of Jesus

Some will declare that Jesus was a completely invented personage, and that the man never really existed. This is another argument that I find rather flimsy in nature. Consider this: If the Romans had faced significant challenges with the early Christians, would it not have been easier to discredit the movement by proving that Jesus never existed? Would it not make sense to question why the Disciples and many early Christians endured severe torture and execution if Jesus had never existed? So, would one conceive that these people, most likely, would not have subjected themselves to such arduous punishment if the man had really never existed? Would you? However, let us look at some of the most common arguments against the historicity of Jesus.

Of course, everyone is familiar with the New Testament Bible, which details many aspects of the life, death, and resurrection of Jesus the Nazarene, who was called the Christ. There has been no other character in history who has had his life's biography as translated and well dispersed as this one man. Yet, many will claim that since these are "religious" writings they cannot be counted on as definitive proof that the man actually existed. This even though most people have no problem accepting the existence of people like Alexander the Great, who had nowhere near the amount of original literature.

Lack of Contemporary Evidence

Many people will point to the absence of contemporary Roman records, or writings directly referencing Jesus. They will say that major historians like Josephus and Tacitus only mention Jesus briefly, and these references are often considered secondary sources written decades after Jesus' death. But is this truly the case? We must remember that, in the first century, most people could not read or write, including the people closest to Jesus. Most of his closest confidants were fishermen, with no real education. So, we cannot expect for them to have directly recorded, in written word, what Jesus said and did. In fact, literacy in large numbers has only been a recent accomplishment in human history.

According to modern mainstream historical thought, the earliest forms of writing emerged around 3200 BC in Mesopotamia with cuneiform script, and in Egypt with hieroglyphics. However, literacy was limited to a small elite class, including scribes, priests, and rulers. In ancient Greece and Rome, literacy rates were higher among the elite, but the majority of the population remained illiterate. Education was typically restricted to wealthy males. During the Middle Ages, literacy rates were low. Most people were illiterate, with literacy confined mainly to clergy, monks, and a small educated elite. Monasteries became centers of learning and manuscript preservation.

The Renaissance of the 14th to 17th centuries marked a revival of learning and education, particularly in Europe. The invention of the printing press, by Johannes Gutenberg in the mid-15th century, revolutionized the spread of information and books, gradually increasing literacy rates. The Protestant Reformation, in the 16th century, emphasized the importance of reading religious texts. This contributed to the growth of literacy as people sought to read the Bible in their vernacular languages. However, prior to this period, literacy was limited to only a very few privileged people.

Therefore, it was still very common in the first century for information to be passed along orally, rather than in written text. So, knowing this, would one really expect to find many non-biblical written texts about a carpenter from Nazareth? Well, let us look for some non-biblical pagan accounts of Jesus in the historical records, because these people would have generally been fairly hostile to Christianity.

Some authors denied the miraculous nature of Jesus. *Thallus* (52 AD) is perhaps the earliest secular author to mention Jesus when he attempted to explain away the darkness occurring during the crucifixion of Jesus. About this subject, Thallus said, "*On the whole world there pressed a most fearful **darkness**; and the rocks were rent by an **earthquake**, and many places in **Judea** and other districts were thrown down.*" In the third book of his called *History* Thallus calls, "*as appears to me without reason, an **eclipse of the sun**.*" (Julius Africanus, *Chronography*, 18:1)

Cornelius Tacitus (56-120 AD), one of the most reliable ancient historians, was well-regarded for his detailed examination of historical records. In the *Annals* written around 116 AD[9] Tacitus provides an account of Emperor Nero's reaction to the great fire of Rome, where Nero placed the blame on the Christians. Tacitus' account offers a brief but crucial mention of Jesus (referred to as "**Christus**") and the persecution of early Christians during Nero's rule.

Mara Bar-Serapion, a Syrian philosopher writing around 70 AD[10], addressed a letter to his son that compared the persecution of Jesus with the mistreatment of other philosophers who faced condemnation for their beliefs. His letter provides significant historical value, as it acknowledges Jesus as a real person with profound influence, referring to him as the "*Wise King*." Bar-Serapion writes: "*Or the Jews by murdering their **wise king**?… After that, their kingdom was abolished. God rightly avenged these men… The **wise king**… Lived on in the teachings he enacted.*" This underscores the enduring legacy of Jesus and aligns him with other respected figures of wisdom.

Julius Africanus (80-140 AD) refers to a historian named Phlegon, who documented a series of historical events around 140 AD[11]. Phlegon notably mentions the period of darkness surrounding the crucifixion of

---

[9] Cornelius Tacitus, Annals 15.44.
[10] Mara Bar-Serapion, *Letter to His Son*, in F.F. Bruce, *Jesus and Christian Origins Outside the New Testament* (Grand Rapids, MI: Eerdmans Publishing, 1974), 30-32.
[11] Julius Africanus, *Chronography*, 18:1, quoted in *Origen, Contra Celsum* 2.14.

Jesus, attempting to provide a natural explanation for the phenomenon. Africanus quotes Phlegon: *"Phlegon records that, in the time of Tiberius Caesar, at full moon, there was a full **eclipse of the sun** from the sixth to the ninth hour."* This description aligns with accounts of an unusual darkness during the crucifixion, suggesting that even secular historians of the time took note of these extraordinary events.

Phlegon was also mentioned by *Origen* when he said, *"Now Phlegon, in the thirteenth or fourteenth book, I think, of his Chronicles, not only ascribed to **Jesus** a knowledge of future events . . . but also testified that the result corresponded to His predictions."* (Origen *Against Celsus*, Book 2, Chapter 14[12])

*"And with regard to the **eclipse** in the time of Tiberius Caesar, in whose reign **Jesus** appears to have been crucified, and the great **earthquakes** which then took place ... "* (Origen *Against Celsus*, Book 2, Chapter 33)

*"**Jesus**, while alive, was of no assistance to himself, but that he **arose after death**, and exhibited the marks of his punishment, and showed how his **hands** had been **pierced** by nails."* (Origen *Against Celsus*, Book 2, Chapter 59)

Pliny the Younger (61-113 AD), in a letter to the Roman emperor Trajan[13], describes the lifestyles of early Christians: *"They (the **Christians**) were in the habit of meeting on a certain fixed day before it was light when they sang in alternate verses a hymn to **Christ**, as to a god, and bound themselves by a solemn oath, not to any wicked deeds, but never to commit any fraud, theft, or adultery, never to falsify their word, nor deny a trust when they should be called upon to deliver it up; after which it was their custom to separate, and then reassemble to partake of food—but food of an ordinary and innocent kind."*

---

[12] Origen, *Against Celsus*, Book 2, Chapter 14.
[13] Pliny the Younger, *Letters*, Book 10, Letter 96.

Suetonius (69-140 AD), a Roman historian who served as an annalist of the Imperial House under Emperor Hadrian, provides notable accounts of early Christians. He describes the actions taken by Emperor Claudius (41-54 AD), stating: *"Because the Jews at Rome caused constant disturbances at the instigation of **Chrestus** (Christ), he (Claudius) expelled them from the city (Rome)."*[14] This expulsion took place in 49 AD.

Lucian of Samosata (115-200 AD), a Greek satirist, spoke with sarcasm about Christ and Christians, yet he implicitly acknowledged their existence by never referring to them as fictional. He commented[15]: *"The **Christians**, you know, worship a man to this day— the distinguished personage who introduced their novel rites and was **crucified** on that account..."* Then he goes on further to describe that his followers *"worship the **crucified sage**, and live after his laws. All this they take quite on faith, with the result that they **despise all worldly goods** alike, regarding them merely as **common property**."*

Celsus, writing around 175 AD, presented a critical account of Jesus, suggesting a controversial narrative about his origins[16]: *"**Jesus** had come from a village in **Judea**, and was the son of a poor Jewess... **Jesus**, on account of his poverty, was hired out to go to **Egypt**. While there, he acquired certain (magical) powers which Egyptians pride themselves on possessing. He returned home highly elated at **possessing these powers**, and on the strength of them gave himself out to be a god."*

Flavius Josephus (37-101 AD), a Jewish historian, made one of the earliest non-Christian references to Jesus in *The Antiquities of the Jews* written around 93 AD[17]: *"Now around this time lived **Jesus**, a wise man. For he was a worker of **amazing deeds** and was a teacher of people who gladly accept the truth. He won over both many Jews*

---

[14] Suetonius, *The Lives of the Caesars: The Life of Claudius*, 25:4.
[15] Lucian of Samosata, *The Death of Peregrine*, 11-13.
[16] Celsus, *The True Doctrine*, quoted in Origen, *Against Celsus*, Book 1, Chapter 32.
[17] Flavius Josephus, *The Antiquities of the Jews*, Book 18, Chapter 3.

and many Greeks. Pilate, when he heard him accused by the leading men among us, **condemned** *him to the* **cross**."

Conclusion

Therefore, I contend that, based on the above accounts of Jesus and the early Christians, at least the historicity of Jesus must be considered verified. Also, based on these same accounts, we can consider it verified that many of the claims of the biblical texts were actually understood to be common claims of his day as well. Now, whether these claims were true or not is another thing altogether, which must remain in the realms of personal faith. Thus, I do believe we should now be able to consider at least the historicity of the man to be valid, as well as many of the claims and historical events.

However, it is my desire that by the time we reach the end of this book you will see the true nature of Christ as the purveyor of Truth and Consciousness that he was. Yet, we must first deal with the false truths that were conceptualized and birthed by the Empire as a means of controlling the populus. Thus, in the next chapter we will dive headfirst into the quagmire that was created by Rome.

Chapter-2: The Suppression of Knowledge

The Truth About the Bible

Fear has no place in a faith rooted in Divine Love. History has shown us that fear has been one of the greatest tools used to control people throughout time. However, we now find ourselves in an era where truth is emerging in its purest form, encouraging each of us to let go of fear and discover the powerful love that Christ embodied. When we focus on His teachings, we find that fear only obscures the message. But God's truth brings clarity, peace, and a love that casts out all fear.

In our age of social media and digital interactions, we can sometimes forget the value of true personal connection. This is where the local church holds a unique role, offering a space for fellowship and spiritual growth among like-minded people. As Jesus taught, *"Where **two or more** are gathered in my name, there **I am** also"*. A loving hug and a kind word shared in person carry a depth and sincerity that no emoji can replace, providing us with strength and a sense of unity. Thus, the local church can be a community of shared faith where people gather in love and mutual support.

For this to happen in today's age of disillusionment with the current doctrinal belief systems, the church must abandon the false message of fear, and embrace the True teachings of Christ which are based in total unconditional Love. Whether they realize it or not, most pastors in the Christian church today are leading from a place of fear. This is due, in large part, to the rapidly declining numbers of people in their churches each and every week. Thus, they feel that they must preach hellfire and damnation in order to keep the people that still remain locked in by fear. However, in actuality nothing could be further from the truth! People are longing for the message of Love and acceptance that Christ embodied.

As we explore the Bible's history and purpose, we encourage every reader, including pastors and leaders, to seek this truth for themselves. I invite you to seek guidance from the Spirit on these matters, as you read through this book. In fact, you should consider it an act of faith to ask God to reveal truth and to grant the wisdom to see past fear and judgment. Focus instead on divine love and unity, which were at the very heart of Christ's message.

In sharing this invitation, we want to make clear that the critiques and explorations in this chapter come not from a place of judgment, but from a desire to move closer to the True concept of Love that Christ taught. For God IS Love and Light, and love is the opposite of hate. Hate is fueled by fear, but truth, Divine Truth, is the antidote to fear! Thus truth will help us all to embrace a higher path rooted in compassion, courage, and wisdom. For in the immortal words of Jesus Christ, *"If you abide in my word, you are truly my disciples, and you* **will know the truth,** *and the* **truth will set you free.***"*

The History of the Bible

Regardless of personal beliefs, it is impressive that the Bible remains the most widely read book throughout recorded history. Each year, an estimated 100 million copies are sold worldwide, with 20 million sold in the United States alone[18]. Given its immense popularity and lasting impact, it is essential to take a closer look at the "holy scriptures" to understand why they have captivated readers and scholars for the past 2,000 years.

What exactly is "The Bible," and where did it come from? If you ask a committed believer, they may say the Bible is the "Inerrant Word of God," intended to guide humanity toward truth and teach us how to live. However, many are unaware that the Bible is actually a compilation of over 65 individual books. The total number varies depending on the specific version: the Protestant Bible contains 66 books, the Catholic Bible has 73, and Orthodox Bibles can include anywhere from 79 to 86 books. The texts were written in three languages, including Hebrew, Aramaic, and Greek, across three continents: Europe, Africa, and Asia. It is widely accepted that around

---

[18] James Chapman, *The World's Most Popular Books*, ResearchGate, 2014.

forty different authors contributed to the Bible's writing over a span of around 1,500 years[19].

The astute reader might well ask themselves, how could a collection of books written over such a long time by so many different authors be considered the true "Inerrant Word of God"? And why are there so many different versions of the Bible? Are they all the true "Word of God"? If so, why are some books left out of different versions? Let us examine the history of the Bible, and perhaps some of these questions may be answered in the process.

The Bible consists of what is considered the "Old Testament" and the "New Testament." The Old Testament is a collection of books of the Hebrew Bible called the Tanakh. It consists of the first five books called the Jewish Torah, the books that tell the history of the Israelites, the poetic and wisdom books, and finally, the books of the prophets, which warn of the consequences of turning away from God. The New Testament deals primarily with the person of Jesus, his life, and his ministry, as well as the lives of the disciples and the early years of the Christian church in the first century. There was about a 400-year gap between the writings of the Old Testament and the New Testament, and the New was considered by Christians to be a continuation and completion of the Old. Jesus himself claimed to be the fulfillment of the Old Testament when he said:

Matthew 5:17 - *"Do not think that I came to **destroy the Law** or the Prophets. I didn't come to destroy them, but to **fulfill them**."*

Rome and the Council of Nicaea

The Roman Empire occupied and controlled Israel from 63 BC until the first Jewish revolt in 66 AD, when Jewish forces temporarily expelled the Romans. However, Rome swiftly recaptured Jerusalem in 70 AD, destroying the Temple and dispersing the Jewish population

---

[19] John Barton, *A History of the Bible: The Book and Its Faiths* (New York: Viking, 2019), 120–125.

throughout the Empire[20]. During this period, both Jews and the emerging Christian communities presented significant challenges for the Romans, particularly in the first four centuries of occupation. In response, Christians faced severe persecution as Roman authorities attempted to eradicate the new faith. Christian worship gatherings were strictly banned, and individuals who refused to renounce their faith were stripped of legal rights, subjected to flogging, or even executed.[21]

The Roman Emperor Constantine's conversion to Christianity is often viewed more as a political strategy to unite the Roman Empire, rather than a purely spiritual transformation. Nonetheless, Constantine's declaration of Christianity as Rome's official religion marked the foundation of what would later become the Holy Roman Empire. In 325 AD, he convened the First Council of Nicaea to establish an official Roman doctrine of Christianity and to decide which texts would be included in the canonical Bible. As a result, many early Christian writings were excluded from the canon, labeled as heretical, and subsequently destroyed. The suppression of alternative views and the selection of specific texts gave Rome and the newly established Roman Catholic Church complete control over the Christian religion, solidifying a unified doctrine that aligned with imperial interests.[22]

Many of these so-called heretical texts were believed to be lost forever. Then, in 1945, a treasure trove of ancient manuscripts was found by a local farmer in clay jars near the Upper Egyptian town of Nag Hammadi[23]. These included many of the early Christian books thought to have been lost to history, such as the **Apocryphon of**

---

[20] Simon Sebag Montefiore, *Jerusalem: The Biography* (New York: Knopf, 2011), 172-180.

[21] W.H.C. Frend, *Martyrdom and Persecution in the Early Church: A Study of Conflict from the Maccabees to Donatus* (New York: Oxford University Press, 1965), 469-475.

[22] Jaroslav Pelikan, *The Christian Tradition: A History of the Development of Doctrine, Volume 1: The Emergence of the Catholic Tradition (100-600)* (Chicago: University of Chicago Press, 1971), 79-83.

[23] James M. Robinson, ed., *The Nag Hammadi Library* (San Francisco: Harper & Row, 1988), xxiii-xxv.

James, *The Gospel of Truth*, *The Apocryphon of John*, *The Gospel of Thomas*, the *Treatise of Melchizedek*, as well as forty-five other texts. Most of these were considered to be Gnostic gospels, derived from a group of early Christians who claimed to have secret knowledge about the universe, Christ, and his appearance on earth. Gnosticism was a diverse and influential religious and philosophical movement that emerged in the early centuries of the Christian era. The term "Gnosticism" is derived from the Greek word *gnosis*, meaning "knowledge." Gnostics believed that salvation could be attained through special, esoteric knowledge of spiritual truths and divine realities, which they claimed were hidden from the ordinary believer.[24]

However, there were other books also not included in the official canonized Bible, such as the **Book of Enoch**[25], which is only found in the Ethiopian Bible. This book contains unique materials on the origins of demons and the Nephilim, why some angels fell from heaven, an explanation of the Genesis Flood, and prophecy about the thousand-year reign of the Messiah.

Few recognize that although the Roman Empire ceased as a political entity, its influence persisted through the establishment of the Roman Catholic Church. Although the official "governing" body of Rome collapsed, the influence that the Roman Catholic Church has continued to have on society as the "Holy Roman Empire" has probably been even greater than did the official governmental structure. Just consider the words in the "Apostles' Creed" which state, "*I believe in...the* **holy Catholic Church**..."

Many Christians recite prayers every Sunday without realizing that they are still honoring what remains of the Roman Empire, which places the Pope as an intermediary between them and God. Over the past 2,000 years, the Roman Catholic Church has been responsible for some of history's greatest atrocities, including the persecution and

---

[24] Elaine Pagels, *The Gnostic Gospels* (New York: Vintage Books, 1979), 34-38, 68-73.
[25] R.H. Charles, ed., *The Book of Enoch* (Oxford: Clarendon Press, 1912), xvii-xxi.

suppression of entire cultures in the name of Jesus Christ, distorting the original teachings of Yeshua beyond recognition.

The exclusion of alternative perspectives and texts in the formation of the canonical Bible reflects a broader effort to consolidate a unified narrative of Christianity. This effort extended to the very texts that were preserved, as certain translations and edits reflect ideological influences designed to align with prevailing power structures.

Biblical Edits

Many assert that the Bible has been altered throughout history to serve the interests of those in power. As we've already discussed, the Roman Catholic Church condemned and burned numerous texts they labeled "heretical" during the First Council of Nicaea in 325 AD. This practice of destruction was not limited to early Christian writings, as the Catholic Church has a well-documented history of eradicating cultural and religious texts worldwide. One notable example occurred during the Spanish conquest, when thousands of Mayan manuscripts were burned[26]. Many of these documents contained incredibly valuable scientific knowledge of which the conquistadors could not have possibly comprehended. The Mayans, deeply distressed, wept as they watched their heritage being destroyed, while the conquistadors, lacking both the understanding and interest, dismissed the significance of these works.

Aside from that, were there other "edits" that were made to the biblical texts that were kept by the Romans? Well, certainly there were many differences in interpretation and translation from one language to another, but for the most part, the biblical texts adopted by the Roman Catholic Church have maintained their congruency over the centuries since. However, there are a few examples where there have been obvious modifications to mold the texts to certain ideological perspectives.

---

[26] Diego de Landa, *Relacion de las Cosas de Yucatan*, trans. William Gates (Baltimore: The Maya Society, 1937), 18-21.

Most people have at least heard of the "King James Version" (KJV) of the Bible. However, many might not realize that an earlier English version, the "Geneva Bible," was actually the most widely distributed and influential Bible of the 16th century. Renowned authors like William Shakespeare, John Bunyan, and John Milton frequently cited the Geneva Bible in their works. This version was even brought to the Americas on the Mayflower's maiden voyage. Despite its popularity, the Geneva Bible was not well received by everyone. King James I strongly disapproved of it, going so far as to ban the text in 1616. He believed it contained "*seditious*" ideas and fostered "*dangerous and traitorous conceits.*"[27] Interestingly, the KJV, commissioned by King James and published in 1611, largely followed the same basic translation as the Geneva Bible. This invites an examination of King James' strong opposition to the Geneva Bible.

There were a few marked differences between the KJV and the GNV Bibles, such as the following:

John 1:12

- KJV: *But as many as received him, to them gave he power **to become** the **sons of God**, even to them that believe on his name*:
- GNV: *But as many as received him, to them he gave prerogative **to be** the **sonnes of God**, even to them that believe in his Name.*

One could contend that in the above passage, the King preferred the concept of being given "*power **to become***" over simply "*prerogative **to be**,*" because prerogative to be implies that they already were sons of God while granting power to become implies they were not previously..

John 14:2

---

[27] Gordon Campbell, *Bible: The Story of the King James Version, 1611-2011* (Oxford: Oxford University Press, 2010), 67-72.

- KJV: *In my Father's house are many **mansions**: if it were not so, I would have told you. I go to prepare a place for you.*
- GNV: *In my Fathers house are many **dwelling places**: if it were not so, I would have told you: I go to prepare a place for you.*

In **John 14:2**, one could argue that King James preferred the idea of promising the people "***mansions***" over mere "***dwelling places***." However, one would hardly expect minimalistic items such as these to justify an official banning of the Geneva Bible. Yet there is another difference between the two versions that might justify the King's actions in his mind. In the book of Ephesians, chapter 6, verse 12, we have a fairly well-known verse, whether you are a devout Christian or not:

Ephesians 6:12

- KJV: *For we wrestle not against flesh and blood, but against principalities, against powers, against the **rulers of the darkness** of this world, against spiritual wickedness **in high places**.*
- GNV: *For we wrestle not against flesh and blood, but against principalities, against powers, and against the **worldly governors**, the **princes of the darkness** of this world, against spiritual wickedness, which are **in the high places**.*

Naturally, King James would not have wanted this verse to state "*against the **worldly governors***," as it could have been interpreted as a direct challenge to his authority as a monarch. The last difference is a bit more subtle in nature. By removing the comma and combining the last two sections together, it rendered "*against spiritual wickedness in high places*," rather than stating that all of the named opponents (i.e. - principalities, powers, worldly governors, princes, and wickedness) were "*in high places*". How much higher a place could one be than the King's Throne? This example certainly challenges the notion that the King James Version is the most accurate translation of the Bible.

However, that being said, the canonized New Testament has more ancient manuscripts available for comparison than any other ancient work of literature, with over 66,000 scrolls and manuscripts in total. Thus, for the most part, we can say that the core texts of the canonized Bible have come down to us today primarily intact, more or less as it was in the 4th century. The New Testament books you read today are, by and large, the same documents that were read in the early centuries. Now, the meaning behind those texts might be another question altogether.

While questions about the textual integrity of the Bible remain, archaeology offers a different lens through which to evaluate its historical reliability. By uncovering tangible evidence of people, places, and events described in the scriptures, these discoveries invite us to explore the intersection of faith, history, and the enduring impact of sacred texts.

The Historicity of the Bible

There have been several archaeological findings that support and illuminate biblical narratives, providing historical context and evidence for events, places, and figures mentioned in the Bible. While archaeology does not always provide direct proof of biblical stories, it often confirms the historical and cultural backdrop against which these narratives took place. Although archaeology cannot validate the theological claims of the Bible, it provides valuable evidence supporting historical events, locations, and figures, enriching our understanding of the ancient world. Following are some examples of archaeological finds which lend credence to the historicity of the Bible in general.

The El Arish Stone

In the small Isma'ilya Museum near Cairo lies an extraordinary artifact known as the El Arish Stone, a piece of black granite weighing over two tons and inscribed with hieroglyphics. Its inscriptions tell a tale set around 1500 BC, that appears to parallel the Biblical account of the Exodus. Remarkably, the story is recounted from the perspective of the Egyptian Pharaoh, providing a rare and provocative glimpse into how the events may have been recorded by the Egyptians themselves.

The hieroglyphs describe the "parting of the sea" using a unique symbol of three waves and two knives, which some Egyptologists interpret as a literal reference to the parting waters described in Exodus 14. The narrative also aligns with other key elements of the Exodus, including references to prolonged darkness, a tempest, and the Israelites' encampment near a place called "Pekharti," identified as Pi-hahiroth in the Torah. This artifact, with its striking parallels and Egyptian perspective, serves as a powerful piece of evidence supporting the Bible's historicity, while also inviting deeper exploration into the cultural and historical memory of one of history's most pivotal events.

The Merneptah Stele

The Merneptah Stele[28], also called the Israel Stele or the Victory Stele of Merneptah, is an ancient Egyptian inscription dating to the reign of Pharaoh Merneptah, who ruled Egypt from around 1213 to 1203 BC. Measuring about 7.5 feet tall and 3.4 feet wide, the inscription is carved in Egyptian hieroglyphics. It contains the earliest known reference to "Israel" outside of the Bible. Made of black granite, the stele features a poetic account of Pharaoh Merneptah's military victories in Canaan and Libya. The most notable aspect of the Merneptah Stele is its mention of "*Israel*" among the defeated peoples, with the inscription stating: "*Israel is laid waste, its seed is no more.*" This represents the earliest known reference to Israel as a distinct group in Canaan, providing crucial insights into the early history of the Israelites.

The Tel Dan Inscription

---

[28] James K. Hoffmeier, *Israel in Egypt: The Evidence for the Authenticity of the Exodus Tradition* (Oxford: Oxford University Press, 1997), 32-36.

The Tel Dan Inscription[29], also called the "House of David" Stele, was discovered in 1993 at the archaeological site of Tel Dan in northern Israel. This Aramaic inscription dates back to the 9th century BC and makes reference to the "House of David," indicating the dynasty of King David, a prominent biblical figure. The inscription offers the earliest known extra-biblical mention of King David, providing evidence for the existence of a Davidic dynasty in ancient Israel. This discovery lends support to the biblical narratives found in the Books of Samuel and Kings, which describe the historical lineage of David.

The Mesha Stele

The Mesha Stele, also referred to as the Moabite Stone, was uncovered in 1868 in Dhiban, Jordan. This basalt stone dates back to approximately 840 BC and was created under the reign of Mesha, the king of Moab. The inscription details Mesha's victories against Israel and makes mention of the "House of Omri," referencing the Israelite king Omri[30]. The Mesha Stele aligns with the biblical account in **2 Kings 3**, which narrates a conflict between Moab and Israel. It provides a Moabite perspective on the events, further confirming the existence of the Omride dynasty in ancient Israel.

The Siloam Inscription

The Siloam Inscription was discovered in 1880 in the Siloam Tunnel in Jerusalem. This Hebrew inscription dates to the 8th century BC and describes the construction of the tunnel, which was part of King Hezekiah's efforts to secure Jerusalem's water supply during an Assyrian siege. The inscription aligns with the biblical account in **2 Kings 20:20** and **2 Chronicles 32:30**[31], which describe Hezekiah's

---

[29] Avraham Biran and Joseph Naveh, "An Aramaic Stele Fragment from Tel Dan," *Israel Exploration Journal* 43, no. 2/3 (1993): 81-98.
[30] André Lemaire, "The Mesha Stele and the Omri Dynasty," *Biblical Archaeology Review* 20, no. 3 (1994): 30-37.
[31] Nahman Avigad, *Discovering Jerusalem* (Nashville: Thomas Nelson, 1983), 101-104.

tunnel project. It provides tangible evidence of Hezekiah's reign and his engineering achievements in Jerusalem.

The Cyrus Cylinder

The Cyrus Cylinder was discovered in 1879 in Babylon, which is modern-day Iraq, and dates to the 6th century BC[32]. This clay cylinder contains an inscription by Cyrus the Great, proclaiming his conquest of Babylon and his policy of allowing exiled peoples to return to their homelands. The cylinder corroborates the biblical account of the Jewish exiles returning from Babylonian captivity, as described in the book of *Ezra*. Cyrus's decree allowed the Jews to rebuild the Temple in Jerusalem, marking a pivotal moment in Jewish history.

The Lachish Letters

The Lachish Letters, unearthed in 1935 at the ancient city of Lachish in Israel[33], consist of inscribed pottery shards dating back to the late 7th century BC. These letters contain messages exchanged between military officials during the Babylonian siege of Lachish. They offer a vivid, firsthand account of the anxiety and turmoil faced during the invasion, aligning with the events described in the book of *Jeremiah*. The contents of these letters shed light on the political tensions in Judah, corroborating the historical backdrop of the biblical narrative.

The Pool of Siloam

The Pool of Siloam, uncovered in 2004 in the City of David[34] Jerusalem, dates back to the time of Jesus. It is referenced in the Gospel of John as the place where Jesus performed the miracle of healing a man who was blind from birth, as described in **John 9:1-11**. This discovery affirms the historical existence of the Pool of Siloam as

---

[32] Amélie Kuhrt, *The Persian Empire: A Corpus of Sources from the Achaemenid Period* (London: Routledge, 2007), 70-75.

[33] Harry Torczyner (Naftali Herz Tur-Sinai), *The Lachish Letters* (Oxford: Oxford University Press, 1938), 14-20.

[34] Ronny Reich and Eli Shukron, "*The Discovery of the Siloam Pool in Jerusalem,*" Biblical Archaeology Review 31, no. 5 (2005): 22-27.

a significant site in Jerusalem during the Second Temple period, corroborating the New Testament account.

The City of David

Excavations in the City of David, the oldest section of Jerusalem, have uncovered structures and artifacts dating back to the era of King David and Solomon[35]. The findings include fortifications, large buildings, and inscriptions that align with the biblical narrative of Jerusalem as the capital of the united monarchy. These archaeological discoveries provide evidence for the historical presence of a prominent city during the period traditionally associated with David and Solomon, as described in the books of *Samuel* and *Kings*.

Hezekiah's Wall

The Broad Wall[36], attributed to King Hezekiah, was uncovered in the Jewish Quarter of Jerusalem. This impressive defensive structure, dating to the 8th century BC, is referenced in the Bible as part of Hezekiah's measures to prepare for an Assyrian siege (**2 Chronicles 32:5**). The discovery of this wall offers tangible evidence of Jerusalem's fortifications during Hezekiah's reign and corroborates the biblical narrative of his efforts to safeguard the city.

These archaeological findings provide tangible evidence that supports and contextualizes various biblical narratives. So again, while archaeology cannot prove the theological claims of the Bible, it does help corroborate historical events, places, and figures, enhancing our understanding of the ancient world and its impact on biblical history.

---

[35] Eilat Mazar, *The Palace of King David: Excavations at the Summit of the City of David* (Jerusalem: Shoham Academic Research and Publication, 2009), 15-22.

[36] Nahman Avigad, *Discovering Jerusalem* (Nashville: Thomas Nelson, 1983), 91-95.

Issues with the Old Testament

The following is a verse from the Old Testament where the prophet Jeremiah addresses the people of Judah and the religious leaders and scholars. He criticizes the corrupt and misleading interpretations of the Law by these scribes, who claim to possess wisdom because they have the Law of the Lord. However, Jeremiah points out that their writings have been falsified or twisted, leading the people astray.

Jeremiah 8:8 (NIV): "*How can you say, 'We are wise, for we have the law of the Lord,' when actually the **lying pen** of the scribes has handled it **falsely**?*"

Jeremiah warned that the people of Judah had a false sense of security, believing that merely possessing the Law and the Temple would grant them special protection. He cautioned against relying on these outward symbols without true faith and obedience to God's commands, suggesting that such misplaced confidence would lead to their downfall. Some interpret this verse as a critique of relying solely on human interpretations of religious texts, hinting that even those responsible for preserving sacred writings could be fallible or corrupt. Jeremiah's use of the phrase, "*the **lying pen** of the scribes has handled it **falsely**,*" suggests that awareness of false writings existed even in his time. It highlights the need for genuine understanding and wisdom, rather than unquestioning trust in religious authorities.[37]

Let us now examine some of the "anomalies" in the Old Testament writings.

Deuteronomy

The Book of Deuteronomy is the fifth book of the Torah and the Christian Old Testament, containing laws, speeches, and narratives attributed to Moses. While Deuteronomy is foundational for understanding Jewish law and theology, some of its stories and teachings have been seen as problematic when compared to the

---

[37] Michael L. Brown, *Jeremiah: A Commentary Based on Ancient Jewish and Christian Sources* (Peabody, MA: Hendrickson Publishers, 2010), 115-118.

teachings of Jesus in the New Testament. Following are a few examples.

The Command to Destroy the Canaanites

Deuteronomy 7:1-6 - *When the Lord your God brings you into the land you are entering to possess and drives out before you many nations—the Hittites, Girgashites, Amorites, Canaanites, Perizzites, Hivites, and Jebusites, seven nations larger and stronger than you— and when the Lord your God has delivered them over to you and you have defeated them, then **you must destroy them totally**. Make no treaty with them, and **show them no mercy**. Do not intermarry with them. Do not give your daughters to their sons or take their daughters for your sons, for they will turn your children away from following me to serve other gods, and **the Lord's anger** will burn against you and will quickly **destroy you**. This is what you are to do to them: Break down their altars, smash their sacred stones, cut down their Asherah poles and burn their idols in the fire.*

Deuteronomy 20:16-18 - *However, in the cities of the nations the Lord your God is giving you as an inheritance, **do not leave alive anything that breathes**. Completely destroy them—the Hittites, Amorites, Canaanites, Perizzites, Hivites, and Jebusites—as the Lord your God has commanded you. Otherwise, they will teach you to follow all the detestable things they do in worshiping their gods, and you will sin against the Lord your God.*

Here, the Israelites are commanded by God to completely destroy the Canaanites and other inhabitants of the Promised Land, showing them no mercy. This includes any animals there when it says, "***do not leave alive anything that breathes***." However, this conflicts with the words of Jesus when he taught love for one's enemies, compassion, and mercy. For example, in the Sermon on the Mount, Jesus says:

Matthew 5:43-48 - *"You have heard that it was said, 'Love your neighbor and hate your enemy.' But I tell you, **love your enemies and pray for those who persecute you**, that you may be children of your Father in heaven. **He causes his sun to rise on the evil and the***

good and sends rain on the righteous and the unrighteous. If you love those who love you, what reward will you get? Are not even the tax collectors doing that? And if you greet only your own people, what are you doing more than others? Do not even pagans do that? Be perfect, therefore, as your heavenly Father is perfect."

Therefore, the command to annihilate entire populations, including women and children, stands in stark contrast to Jesus' emphasis on loving enemies and extending mercy, raising ethical concerns for many readers. It also shows that Jesus would certainly not have approved of the many atrocities committed by the Holy Roman Empire centuries later, which were all done in his name.

The Law of Retaliation

Deuteronomy 19:16-21 - *If a malicious witness takes the stand to accuse someone of a crime, the two people involved in the dispute must stand in the presence of the Lord before the priests and the judges who are in office at the time. The judges must make a thorough investigation, and if the witness proves to be a liar, giving false testimony against a fellow Israelite, then do to the false witness as that witness intended to do to the other party. You must purge the evil from among you. The rest of the people will hear of this and* **be afraid***, and never again will such an evil thing be done among you.* **Show no pity***: life for life, eye for eye, tooth for tooth, hand for hand, foot for foot.*

This scripture prescribes the principle of an "*eye for an eye,*" and a "*tooth for a tooth,*" a form of retributive justice. This law was intended to ensure proportional punishment and prevent excessive revenge. However, in **Matthew 5:38-39**, Jesus directly challenges this principle, teaching, *"You have heard that it was said, 'Eye for eye, and tooth for tooth.' But I tell you,* **do not resist an evil person***. If anyone slaps you on the right cheek,* **turn** *to them* **the other cheek** *also."* Thus, Jesus' call for non-retaliation and forgiveness contrasts sharply with the legal code in Deuteronomy, which could be seen as endorsing vengeance.

The Treatment of Captive Women

Deuteronomy 21:10-14 - *When you go to war against your enemies and the Lord your God delivers them into your hands and you take captives, if you notice among the captives a beautiful woman and are attracted to her,* **you may take her as your wife**. *Bring her into your home and have her shave her head, trim her nails and put aside the clothes she was wearing when captured. After she has lived in your house and mourned her father and mother for a full month, then you may go to her and be her husband and* **she shall be your wife**. *If you are not pleased with her, let her go wherever she wishes. You must not sell her or treat her as a slave, since you have dishonored her.*

In this scripture, instructions are given for the treatment of female captives taken in war. An Israelite man is allowed to marry a captive woman, but if he is not pleased with her, he must let her go free and not sell her as a slave. However, Jesus often uplifted the dignity and worth of individuals, including women, and emphasized the importance of love and respect in relationships. Thus, the Deuteronomy passage, while providing some protection to captive women, still treats them as objects to be taken and discarded, which contrasts with Jesus' teachings on human dignity and equality.

The Death Penalty for Various Offenses

Deuteronomy 13:6-10 - *If your very own brother, or your son or daughter, or the wife you love, or your closest friend secretly entices you, saying, "Let us go and worship other gods" (gods that neither you nor your ancestors have known, gods of the peoples around you, whether near or far, from one end of the land to the other), do not yield to them or listen to them.* **Show them no pity**. *Do not spare them or shield them.* **You must certainly put them to death**. **Your hand must be the first in putting them to death**, *and then the hands of all the people. Stone them to death because they tried to turn you away from the Lord your God, who brought you out of Egypt, out of the land* *of slavery. Then all Israel will hear and **be afraid**, and no one among you will do such an evil thing again.*

Here, the people of Israel are instructed with regard to people who entice them to worship other gods: "*Show them no pity. Do not spare them or shield them. **You must certainly put them to death**.*" If this was the one true God and creator of all the Universe, then why would he be so jealous of other lowercase "gods," and why would he have to control his people by making them "***be afraid***"? Should not an all-powerful and all-loving Father God be able to teach his people with a more loving paradigm?

Deuteronomy 21:18-21 - *If someone has a stubborn and rebellious son who does not obey his father and mother and will not listen to them when they discipline him, his father and mother shall take hold of him and bring him to the elders at the gate of his town. They shall say to the elders, "This son of ours is stubborn and rebellious. He will not obey us. He is a glutton and a drunkard." Then all the men of his town are to **stone him to death**. You must purge the evil from among you. All Israel will hear of it and **be afraid**.*

This scripture speaks to how the Israelites should deal with a "*stubborn and rebellious*" son. In these cases, the community is instructed to stone the offenders to death! Thankfully, such laws are not the norm today, as they would have severe implications for modern society. Once more, the passage concludes with an emphasis on fear rather than love. This also conflicts with the story of the "Prodigal Son", where the stubborn and rebellious son is actually given his inheritance early. He goes off and wastes it on a sinful existence, and then returns to his father's house to beg for forgiveness. However, the father greets him with love and forgiveness.

In stark contrast, Jesus frequently taught about forgiveness and showed mercy to those condemned by the law. The story of the woman caught in adultery is a key example, where Jesus prevents her from being stoned.

John 8:2-11 - *At dawn he (Jesus) appeared again in the temple courts, where all the people gathered around him, and he sat down to teach them. The teachers of the law and the Pharisees brought in a* **woman caught in adultery**. *They made her stand before the group and said to Jesus, "Teacher, this woman was caught in the act of adultery. In the Law Moses commanded us to* **stone such women**. *Now what do you say?" They were using this question as a trap, in order to have a basis for accusing him. But Jesus bent down and started to write on the ground with his finger. When they kept on questioning him, he straightened up and said to them, "Let any one of you who is without sin be the first to throw a stone at her." Again he stooped down and wrote on the ground. At this, those who heard began to go away one at a time, the older ones first, until only Jesus was left, with the woman still standing there. Jesus straightened up and asked her, "Woman, where are they? Has no one condemned you?" "No one, sir," she said.* **"Then neither do I condemn you**,*" Jesus declared. "Go now and leave your life of sin."*

The harshness of the death penalty in Deuteronomy, especially for offenses like disobedience to parents, seems completely incompatible with Jesus' message of forgiveness and redemption. Thus, I do not believe Jesus would have approved of burning people at the stake as the Holy Roman Empire did many times throughout the centuries following his death. I am absolutely positive that the fact the Empire did these atrocious things in his name made Christ weep.

Exclusion from the Assembly

Deuteronomy 23:1-6 - *No one who has been emasculated by crushing or cutting may enter the assembly of the Lord. No one born of a forbidden marriage nor any of their descendants may enter the assembly of the Lord, not even in the tenth generation. No Ammonite or Moabite or any of their descendants may enter the assembly of the Lord, not even in the tenth generation. For they did not come to meet you with bread and water on your way when you came out of Egypt, and they hired Balaam son of Beor from Pethor in Aram Naharaim to pronounce a curse on you. However, the Lord your God would not listen to Balaam but turned the curse into a blessing for you, because* *the Lord your God loves you.* **Do not seek a treaty of friendship with them as long as you live.**

This scripture contains laws excluding certain groups of people from the assembly of the Lord, including eunuchs, illegitimate children, and certain foreign nations up to the tenth generation. Yet Jesus was known for his inclusive approach, welcoming those who were marginalized, such as tax collectors, sinners, and foreigners. He preached that the Kingdom of God was open to all who believed. Thus, the exclusionary nature of the laws in Deuteronomy contrasts with the inclusive message of Jesus, who broke down barriers between different groups of people.

The Left-Brain of Deuteronomy

The portrayal of God in the book of Deuteronomy significantly contrasts with the image of God presented by Jesus in the New Testament. Betty J. Kovacs, PhD, an author and scholar who earned her doctorate from the University of California, Irvine, in Comparative Literature and Theory of Symbolic/Mythic Language, argues that the Deuteronomists, in 621 BC, dismantled the "marriage" tradition by eliminating the feminine aspect, leaving Yahweh without a feminine co-creator[38]. Interestingly, in various Old Testament scriptures, Yahweh's words seem to imply the existence of multiple "gods," hinting at a more complex divine framework than what is typically acknowledged:

Genesis 1:26 - *"Then God said,* **Let Us** *make man in* **Our** *image, according to* **Our** *likeness; and let them rule over the fish of the sea and over the birds of the sky and over the cattle and over all the earth, and over every creeping thing that creeps on the earth."*

Genesis 3:22 - *And the Lord God said, "The man has now become* **like one of us***, knowing good and evil. He must not be allowed to reach out his hand and take also from the tree of life and eat"*

---

[38] Betty J. Kovacs, *The Miracle of Death: There Is Nothing But Life* (Bloomington, IN: Trafford Publishing, 2003), 45-48.

Genesis 11:7 - "*Come, let **Us** go down and there confuse their language, that they may not understand one another's speech.*"

Deuteronomy 32:8-9 - "*When the Most High gave the nations their inheritance, when He separated the sons of man, He set the boundaries of the peoples according to the number of the **sons of God**. For the Lord's portion is His people; Jacob is the allotment of His inheritance.*"

This verse references the "*sons of God*", suggesting a plurality of divine beings in God's council.

Exodus 15:11 - "*Who is like You **among the gods**, O Lord? Who is like You, majestic in holiness, awesome in praises, working wonders?*"

This verse rhetorically compares Yahweh to other gods, acknowledging their existence but emphasizing Yahweh's supremacy.

Psalm 82:1 - "*God takes His stand in His own congregation; He judges in the midst of the **gods**.*"

This psalm speaks of a divine council, with "gods" (translated from the **plural** Hebrew word **Elohim**) referring to other divine beings or judges.

Psalm 82:6 - "*I said, **You are gods**, and all of you are sons of the Most High.*"

Psalm 89:6-7 - "*For who in the skies is comparable to the Lord? Who among the sons of the mighty is like the Lord, a God greatly feared in the council of the holy ones, and awesome **above all those who are around Him**?*"

This passage refers to a divine council or assembly of heavenly beings, often interpreted as "gods" or "holy ones."

Kovacs believes that all references to the divine feminine were totally destroyed and removed from the texts at this time. As a result the Judaic notion of God became vengeful, violent, and destructive. This view certainly fits within the context of the sections of Deuteronomy that we just covered earlier in this section. The portrayal of God in the book of Deuteronomy certainly contrasts significantly with the image of God presented by Jesus in the New Testament.

The Conquest of Jericho

Joshua 6:16-21 - *The seventh time around, when the priests sounded the trumpet blast, Joshua commanded the army, "Shout! For the Lord has given you the city! The city and all that is in it are to be devoted to the Lord. Only Rahab the prostitute and all who are with her in her house shall be spared because she hid the spies we sent. But keep away from the devoted things, so that you will not bring about your own destruction by taking any of them. Otherwise, you will make the camp of Israel liable to destruction and bring trouble on it.* ***All the silver and gold and the articles of bronze and iron are sacred to the Lord and must go into his treasury.***" *When the trumpets sounded, the army shouted, and at the sound of the trumpet, when the men gave a loud shout, the wall collapsed; so everyone charged straight in, and they took the city. They devoted the city to the Lord and **destroyed with the sword every living thing in it—men and women, young and old, cattle, sheep, and donkeys**.*

The Israelites were under Joshua's leadership at the time, and they were commanded to destroy every living thing in the city of Jericho as part of their conquest of the Promised Land. Only Rahab and her family were spared because she helped the Israelite spies earlier. Notice how they are instructed to keep away from the "*devoted things*" or it would bring about their "*own destruction.*" Yet, they are instructed to bring all the silver and gold and the articles of bronze and iron into the treasury because these things are "*sacred to the Lord.*" So, I guess the command should have been to keep away from the "*devoted things*" that were not made of gold, silver, bronze, or iron?

The Amalekites

1 Samuel 15:2-3 - *This is what the Lord Almighty says: 'I will punish the Amalekites for what they did to Israel when they waylaid them as they came up from Egypt. Now go, attack the Amalekites and totally* *destroy all that belongs to them. Do not spare them;* **put to death men and women, children and infants, cattle and sheep, camels and donkeys***.'"*

Again, God commands the Israelites to utterly destroy the Amalekites, including women, children, infants, and livestock. This command is framed as retribution for an attack the Amalekites made on the Israelites during their exodus from Egypt. However, who could qualify a command to kill all women and children, including infants, as coming from a God of Love? What wrong had the livestock perpetrated on the people of Israel?

The Midianites

Numbers 31:13-18 - *Moses, Eleazar the priest, and all the leaders of the community went to meet them outside the camp. Moses was angry with the officers of the army—the commanders of thousands and commanders of hundreds—who returned from the battle. "Have you allowed all the women to live?" he asked them. "They were the ones who followed Balaam's advice and enticed the Israelites to be unfaithful to the Lord in the Peor incident, so that a plague struck the Lord's people. Now* **kill all the boys. And kill every woman who has slept with a man***, but save for yourselves every* **girl who has never slept with a man***."*

In this passage, Moses was angry with the officers of the army because they had allowed the women and children to live. He commands them to kill all the women and boys, but they could save the young virgin girls for themselves. Does this sound like anything even slightly resembling what would come from a God of Love? One would think not…

The Omnipotence of God

Omnipotence is the attribute of having unlimited power and authority, enabling the ability to do anything that is logically possible. Omnipotence is a property often ascribed to God, signifying His supreme and infinite power over all things. However, this notion leads to what is probably one of the biggest contradictions, in my mind, with reference to the doctrine of Christianity. At least, when taken from the perspective of the dogma of the Empire's religion.

On one hand there is the belief that God is truly omnipotent, all-knowing, all-powerful, and all-good. This would indicate that God knows everything, and has complete control over everything. However, how could an omnipotent God create human beings who for the most part, based on the dogmatic "doctrine" of Christianity, would live out their lives on Earth in a painful and difficult existence, and then the majority of them would be doomed to eternal torment in a place called Hell. This damnation is simply based on the culture to which they were born. That just does NOT equate to a good God in my mind.

More on this later...

Conclusion

Based on the information we have covered in this chapter, I believe we can come away with a couple of major points. First, there is a good amount of archaeological evidence that supports much of the historicity of many of the Old Testament writings as actual historical events. However, I would assert that there are some major conflicts of interest between the God defined in much of the Old Testament writings and the notions of God as painted by the words of Jesus Christ himself. As Betty Kovacs points out, during the formative years of many of the original Old Testament writings there appears to have been a concerted effort to wipe out any notion of the right-brain feminine aspects of the divine nature. Based on my own interpretation of the teachings of Christ, I believe this is one of the things he was trying to correct.

Chapter-3: Other Ancient Texts

There have been many other ancient texts which have told stories similar to those found in the Old Testament. Many of these contain stories about a "Great Flood" cataclysm which was sent by the gods to destroy mankind because they had grown evil. So, let us explore a couple of these and look for similarities.

The Epic of Gilgamesh

The *Epic of Gilgamesh* is one of the oldest known works of literature, originating from ancient Mesopotamia[39]. It consists of a series of Sumerian poems that were eventually compiled into a single epic around the 18th century BC, though the stories themselves likely trace back to much older oral traditions. The most complete version of this epic was discovered in the library of the Assyrian king Ashurbanipal, dating to the 7th century BC. The narrative follows the exploits of Gilgamesh, the king of Uruk, who is described as two-thirds divine and one-third human. As a ruler, Gilgamesh is strong and ambitious but also known for his arrogance and oppressive ways. To counterbalance his behavior, the gods create Enkidu, a wild man who eventually forms a deep friendship with Gilgamesh after a series of dramatic encounters.

Gilgamesh and Enkidu embark on various adventures together, including the defeat of the monster Humbaba in the Cedar Forest and the killing of the Bull of Heaven, sent by the goddess Ishtar. However, Enkidu soon falls ill and dies as punishment from the gods for killing the Bull of Heaven. His death profoundly affects Gilgamesh, leading him to fear his own mortality. Grieving Enkidu's death, Gilgamesh embarks on a quest to find immortality.

Gilgamesh ultimately meets Utnapishtim, who tells him the story of the great flood and informs him that immortality is reserved for the gods. In the flood story, Utnapishtim is the Mesopotamian counterpart to Noah. He is a wise man who survives the great flood and is granted

---

[39] Andrew R. George, *The Epic of Gilgamesh: A New Translation* (London: Penguin Classics, 1999), 1-5.

immortality by the gods. The gods, led by Enlil, decide to exterminate humanity with a catastrophic flood. The reason for this decision is humanity's constant noise and disruption, which disturbs the gods.

Ea, known as the god of wisdom, decides to save Utnapishtim from the flood. He speaks to Utnapishtim in a dream, warning him of the impending flood. Ea instructs Utnapishtim to build a large boat to preserve himself, his family, and the seed of all living creatures. Following Ea's instructions, Utnapishtim constructs a massive boat, making sure it is sealed with bitumen to make it waterproof. The boat is large and strong enough to withstand the floodwaters. Utnapishtim loads the boat with his family, craftsmen, and "*the seed of all living creatures*," essentially ensuring the survival of various species. He also brings gold and other precious items.

The storm and flood waters arrive, unleashed by the gods. The deluge is so powerful that it lasts for six days and nights, submerging the world and destroying everything in its path. On the seventh day, the storm subsides. Utnapishtim's boat comes to rest on a mountain, and he releases a series of birds, including a dove, a swallow, and a raven. The raven does not return, indicating that it has found dry land. Once the floodwaters recede, Utnapishtim disembarks and makes a sacrifice to the gods. The gods, smelling the sweet aroma of the offering, gather around.

Enlil is initially furious that some humans have survived, but Ea intervenes, arguing that exterminating humanity was too harsh. Enlil relents and grants Utnapishtim and his wife immortality as a reward for their piety and wisdom, allowing them to live forever in a distant, peaceful place.

The Eridu Genesis Story

The *Eridu Genesis* is a Sumerian creation myth that dates back to around 1600 BC[40] and is one of the earliest known narratives of its kind. Discovered in fragments on clay tablets, the story describes the

---

[40] Thorkild Jacobsen, *The Harps That Once...: Sumerian Poetry in Translation* (New Haven, CT: Yale University Press, 1987), 148-152.

creation of humanity, the establishment of the first cities, and a devastating flood. The gods, led by Anu, Enlil, Enki, and Ninhursag, create humans from clay to serve as laborers, relieving the gods of their burdensome work. Enki, the god of wisdom and water, and Ninhursag, a goddess associated with fertility, play key roles in forming humanity for this purpose.

Following the creation of humans, the gods establish the first cities, with Eridu recognized as the oldest. Other significant cities include Nippur, Bad-tibira, Sippar, and Shuruppak, which become centers for temple worship and offerings to the gods.

The myth also features a flood narrative, paralleling stories from the *Epic of Gilgamesh* and the biblical account of Noah. In this version, the god Enlil decides to destroy humanity due to their noise and overpopulation. However, Enki intervenes by warning a righteous man named Ziusudra, instructing him to build a large boat to save himself, his family, and the seed of all living things. Ziusudra obeys and, after surviving the flood, offers sacrifices to the gods in gratitude.

The *Eridu Genesis* offers a glimpse into ancient Mesopotamian beliefs about the divine-human relationship, highlighting the dependency of the gods on human labor and the vulnerability of humans to divine actions. The flood narrative serves as a cautionary tale about the consequences of human behavior and underscores the importance of obedience to divine wisdom. This creation myth provides valuable insights into the cultural, religious, and social dynamics of early Mesopotamian society, emphasizing the significance of temple worship and the role of humans as servants to the gods.

The Bible portrays a monotheistic view with a single, all-powerful God, while both the *Epic of Gilgamesh* and the *Eridu Genesis* stories represent polytheistic perspectives, with multiple gods who have different motives and personalities. However, one must consider that in the book of Genesis of the Bible, we do find the following:

Genesis 1:26 - *Then God said, "Let us make mankind in **our image**, in **our** likeness, so that they may rule over the fish in the sea and the* *birds in the sky, over the livestock and all the wild animals, and over all the creatures that move along the ground."*

Genesis 3:22 - *And the Lord God said, "The man has now become like **one of us**, knowing good and evil. He must not be allowed to reach out his hand and take also from the tree of life and eat, and live forever."*

Genesis 11:7 - *"Come, **let Us** go down and there confuse their language, that they may not understand one another's speech."*

Thus, as noted earlier, it would appear that the biblical Genesis also points to the potential for more than one creative entity or "god." However, as also discussed earlier, these are not the only Old Testament scriptures which imply this concept. Actually, if the Old Testament story is taken within the context of the *Eridu Genesis* myth, then the statements above would have proper context if spoken by Anu or Enlil. Enki would have been the "god" who warned Noah about the flood.

It would appear as though, at least with respect to the story of Noah and the flood, that the Old Testament story in Genesis was simply a copy of this original Messapotamian story. The story even originates from the same relative geographical area as the story of Noah's flood. Therefore, it is fairly safe to say that this assumption is accurate. One thing to note is that there is a recurring theme of a global flood catastrophe found in cultures all over the planet. Thus, one must ask if perhaps there is some actual historical validity to the idea of a global catastrophe that has been etched into the collective memory of mankind? This is something I will cover in a future book though, because we have much to cover here, and I do not want us to stray too far from the present task at hand.

Chapter-4: The Concept of Hell

As I sat in church as a child I always wondered how a truly Loving God could create humans as his "children", and then condemn them to eternal damnation and torture in a place called Hell. That never really came across as very "Loving" to me. However, when I would speak to religious "leaders" about this issue, most of them would say that Jesus taught more about Hell than he did any other subject. However...is this actually the case?

Gehenna

First, let us examine the actual original word "Gehenna", most often used by Jesus and the cultural context in his day, which was later translated to "Hell". Gehenna is a term found in the New Testament and occasionally in Jewish literature that has come to be associated with the idea of a place of punishment or a fiery hell. However, its original meaning, and use in scripture, differ significantly from the modern concept of hell as a place of eternal torment.

The term "Gehenna" is derived from the Hebrew "Ge Hinnom," which means the "Valley of Hinnom." This was a valley located just outside of Jerusalem[41]. It is mentioned several times in the Hebrew Bible as a place associated with idolatry and child sacrifice to the pagan deity Molech (e.g., **2 Kings 23:10**, **Jeremiah 7:31**). King Josiah eventually defiled the valley to prevent further sacrifices, and it became infamous as a cursed and unholy place. During the time of Jesus it is believed that Gehenna was used as a garbage dump for Jerusalem, where refuse, animal carcasses, and even criminals' bodies were burned. This led to its association with fire and destruction.

In Jewish religious thought, Gehenna is sometimes seen as a temporary place of purification rather than a permanent state. For many, it was believed to be a place where souls underwent purification

---

[41] Robert W. Funk, *The Acts of Jesus: What Did Jesus Really Do?* (San Francisco: HarperSanFrancisco, 1998), 212–215.

before ultimately being reconciled to God, not a place of eternal damnation[42]. This understanding contrasts sharply with the later Christian notion of an eternal hell. In the time between the Old and New Testaments, Gehenna started to be used metaphorically to describe a place of divine punishment. This concept was embraced in later Jewish thought and appears in the New Testament as a representation of ultimate destruction for the wicked.

Unlike the later Christian conception of hell as a place of eternal, conscious torment, Gehenna as described by Jesus and in Jewish literature is more closely related to destruction and purification. The imagery often used for Gehenna includes fire, which in biblical symbolism represents both judgment and purification. It represents the ultimate consequence of a life lived in rebellion against God. Jesus' teachings on Gehenna were intended to be a wake-up call for his listeners, emphasizing that their actions have spiritual consequences.

Jesus on Hell

Gehenna appears in the New Testament predominantly in the teachings of Jesus in the synoptic Gospels of Matthew, Mark, and Luke. Jesus uses Gehenna to warn about the consequences of sin and disobedience. It is often depicted as a place of fiery judgment, emphasizing the seriousness of moral conduct. However, it is important to remember that in Jesus' time there was no concept of eternal damnation[43]. Below are all of the scriptures in which Jesus talks about Gehenna, which was later translated to the word Hell.

In this first example in **Matthew 5**, it is apparent that Jesus was speaking in regards to judgment of the "court", and as we have already discussed it is believed that the dead corpses of criminals were burned in the fires of Gehenna.

---

[42] Jacob Neusner, *The Theology of the Talmud* (Chicago: University of Chicago Press, 1999), 118–122;

[43] N.T. Wright, *The Resurrection of the Son of God* (Minneapolis: Fortress Press, 2003), 421–425;

Matthew 5:22 - "*But I tell you that anyone who is angry with a brother or sister will be subject to judgment. Again, anyone who says to a brother or sister, 'Raca,' is **answerable to the court**. And anyone who says, 'You fool!' will be in danger of **the fire of hell (Gehenna)**.*"

In the scripture below, it is obvious that Jesus is using this idea as a metaphor, and not literally. For do you really think Jesus expected people to "gouge" out their eye, or "cut off" their hand and throw it away? Yet the Roman Catholic Empire turned this into a literal threat of eternal damnation. You must also remember that this is a continuation of the scripture above where Jesus was talking about court convictions, and we have already seen that they would often burn the bodies of criminals at Gehenna.

Matthew 5:29-30 - "*If your right eye causes you to stumble, **gouge it out and throw it away**. It is better for you to lose one part of your body than for your whole body to be thrown into hell (Gehenna). And if your right hand causes you to stumble, **cut it off and throw it away**. It is better for you to lose one part of your body than for your whole body to **go into hell (Gehenna)**.*"

In **Matthew 10** Jesus was speaking to his disciples about the persecution they would encounter for preaching his message. He was trying to convince them to not fear those who would persecute them, and in doing so he makes the statement in verse 28 as a way to show them that God has the final authority. Thus, the reference to "hell" (Gehenna) in the verse is metaphorical. This reflects the earlier Jewish belief in annihilationism, the idea that souls not reconciled with God are ultimately destroyed in the "Lake of Fire", rather than eternally tormented[44]. Since the disciples were all Jews he was using a metaphor that would resonate with them.

---

[44] James D.G. Dunn, *The New Perspective on Paul* (Grand Rapids: Eerdmans, 2005), 256–259.

Matthew 10:28: "*Do not be afraid of those who kill the body but cannot kill the soul. Rather, be afraid of the One who can **destroy both soul and body in hell (Gehenna)**.*"

The trash heap of Gehenna was seen as an "eternal fire", or a fire that is always burning, because it was a place where the fire seemed perpetual as it was continually being fed with waste and refuse[45]. Thus, Jesus was drawing on that imagery to convey the idea of a complete, ongoing destruction rather than a literal eternity of conscious torment. In that sense, being "thrown into Gehenna" would mean facing a fate as serious and undesirable as being thrown into a trash dump with fires that never ceased to burn. This suggests that Jesus may have been emphasizing the severity and totality of judgment for sin, rather than describing a never-ending punishment in the way that later Christian doctrines have portrayed hell.

Thus in the following scriptures found in **Matthew 18**, by connecting this image to people's everyday experience of the ever-burning trash in Gehenna, Jesus effectively used a familiar and powerful metaphor to communicate the seriousness of sin and its potential outcomes, without necessarily implying eternal conscious torment.

Matthew 18:8-9 - "*If your hand or your foot causes you to stumble, cut it off and throw it away. It is better for you to enter life maimed or crippled than to have two hands or two feet and be thrown into **eternal fire**. And if your eye causes you to stumble, gouge it out and throw it away. It is better for you to enter life with one eye than to have two eyes and be thrown into the **fire of hell (Gehenna)**.*"

In the next two sets of scripture from **Matthew 23**, Jesus was condemning the Pharisees, who were the religious rulers of the day, and ultimately the ones who would have him crucified. By using the words, "*a child of Gehenna*" Jesus was likely drawing an association

---

[45] N.T. Wright, *Jesus and the Victory of God* (Minneapolis: Fortress Press, 1996), 301–305.

between the Pharisees and those of old who practiced child sacrifice to Molech[46].

Matthew 23:15 - *"Woe to you, teachers of the law and Pharisees, you hypocrites! You travel over land and sea to win a single convert, and when you have succeeded, you make them twice as much a **child of hell (Gehenna)** as you are."*

Matthew 23:33 - *"You snakes! You brood of vipers! How will you escape being **condemned to hell (Gehenna)**?"*

The term "*brood of vipers*" implies that these religious leaders are not just corrupt themselves but are the product of a corrupt lineage. It implies an inherited or deep-seated evil, likening them to offspring of snakes. This highlights the idea that their hypocrisy is systemic, not just individual failings, and that their influence is toxic to those they lead.

The quote from Jesus in **Luke 12** below is a retelling of the same thing he said in **Matthew 10:28**, which we already covered above. Thus, this does not count as a separate time when Jesus mentioned "Hell" (Gehenna).

Luke 12:4-5 - *"I tell you, my friends, do not be afraid of those who kill the body and after that can do no more. But I will show you whom you should fear: **Fear** him who, after your body has been killed, has authority to throw you into hell (Gehenna)..."*

In this text, the specific Greek word used that is translated into "fear" is phobēthēte. This word is derived from phobeō, which means "to fear" or "to have reverence." The verb "phobēthēte" in this context implies a strong sense of awe, respect, or fear, typically used when expressing a serious consequence or emphasizing the need to be cautious or fearful of something powerful. Thus, Jesus is instructing his listeners to have

---

[46] Craig S. Keener, *The Gospel of Matthew: A Socio-Rhetorical Commentary* (Grand Rapids: Eerdmans, 2009), 572–576.

a reverential fear of God[47], who has ultimate authority over both physical death and spiritual destiny. This type of fear is an acknowledgment of God's power and authority, rather than a feeling of terror.

The following scriptures in **Mark 9** are a basic retelling of the same sermon Jesus gave in **Matthew 18:8-9**, which we already covered above. So it doesn't count as an additional time Jesus spoke about Hell either.

Mark 9:43-47 - *"If your hand causes you to stumble, cut it off. It is better for you to enter life maimed than with two hands to go into hell (Gehenna), where the fire never goes out. And if your foot causes you to stumble, cut it off. It is better for you to enter life crippled than to have two feet and be thrown into hell (Gehenna)."*

Concept of Eternal Torment

The idea of an eternally tormenting hell does not come directly from the concept of Gehenna as used in scripture but rather from later theological developments in Christianity. Many early Jewish teachings viewed Gehenna as a temporary state, which was a place where souls would be purified for up to a year before either entering paradise or being annihilated. This belief is what Jesus was referring to in the scriptures above. Not a place of eternal torment and damnation.

The imagery of hell we know today has been influenced heavily by non-biblical sources, including *The Divine Comedy* by Dante Alighieri[48] and *Paradise Lost* by John Milton. These literary works, along with the medieval church's focus on hellfire as a means of social control, helped solidify the idea of hell as a place of eternal torment. The concept of hell as eternal punishment was used by religious authorities to instill fear and maintain control over followers. By emphasizing the fear of eternal damnation, the church could influence behaviors and

---

[47] N.T. Wright, *Jesus and the Victory of God* (Minneapolis: Fortress Press, 1996), 452–455.
[48] C.S. Lewis, *The Great Divorce* (New York: Macmillan, 1946), 45–50.

enforce adherence to doctrine, something that did not originate from Jesus' teachings but rather from the evolving dogma of institutionalized Christianity.

Chapter-5: Gnosticism

Gnosticism was a diverse and influential religious and philosophical movement that emerged in the early centuries of the Christian era. The term "Gnosticism" is derived from the Greek word *gnosis*, meaning "knowledge." Gnostics believed that salvation could be attained through special, esoteric knowledge of spiritual truths and divine realities, which they claimed were hidden from the ordinary believer.

Gnostics often viewed the world in dualistic terms, distinguishing sharply between the material and spiritual realms. They considered the material world to be inherently flawed or evil, created by a lesser deity known as the Demiurge, while the true God resided in a higher, spiritual realm. According to Gnostic thought, humans possess a divine spark or soul that originates from the higher spiritual realm. This divine essence is trapped within the physical body and the material world, and the goal of salvation is to awaken this divine spark and return it to its heavenly origin[49].

Gnostics believed that salvation was achieved not through faith alone but through acquiring secret knowledge (gnosis) about one's divine origins and the nature of the cosmos. This knowledge was often transmitted through mystical experiences or teachings from enlightened beings. Gnosticism often stood in contrast to orthodox Christian ideas, challenging traditional doctrines and offering alternative interpretations of Christian teachings. Gnostic texts frequently emphasized personal spiritual experience over institutional authority.

Central to Gnostic belief is the concept of gnosis, or secret knowledge, which leads to salvation. Gnostics taught that enlightenment comes from personal experience and insight into divine truths, mirroring Jesus' focus on inner understanding[50]. Both teachings stress that true

---

[49] Carl G. Jung, *The Gnostic Jung and Other Essays on Psychology and Religion* (Princeton: Princeton University Press, 2002), 45–50.
[50] Elaine Pagels, *The Gnostic Gospels* (New York: Random House, 1979), 92–97.

wisdom and spiritual awakening come from within, advocating for a direct and personal connection to the divine that transcends formal religious structures.

Gnosticism had a significant impact on early Christian thought, prompting theological debates and shaping the development of orthodox doctrine. Although the movement declined after the early centuries primarily due to the creation of Roman Catholicism and its rejection of Gnosticism, its ideas have resurfaced in various religious and philosophical traditions throughout history.

The similarities between the teachings of Jesus and Gnosticism have intrigued scholars and spiritual seekers alike for centuries, sparking debates about the potential influences and shared ideas between these two streams of thought. For instance, Jesus often emphasized the importance of inner spiritual transformation and understanding. In the Gospel of Luke, he states, "*The kingdom of God **is within you***", suggesting a focus on internal, personal discovery rather than external adherence to religious laws.

In the Gospel of John Jesus is frequently associated with light, as seen in statements like, "*I am the **light of the world**. Whoever follows me will never walk in darkness, but will have the **light of life***" in **John 8:12**. This imagery emphasizes illumination and guidance through spiritual truth. Gnostics viewed the material world as a realm of darkness and ignorance, with salvation achieved through the divine light of gnosis. This light was thought to awaken the divine spark within individuals, leading them to their true spiritual home. Thus, both Jesus and Gnostic texts use light as a metaphor for truth and enlightenment, underscoring the transformative power of spiritual insight in overcoming ignorance and darkness.

Jesus often taught about the dangers of the attachment to material wealth, and the importance of spiritual richness. In the Sermon on the Mount of **Matthew 6:19-20**, he warns against storing up treasures on earth, emphasizing that true treasure lies in heaven. Gnostics believed the material world was inherently flawed or evil, and they advocated for a detachment from material possessions to achieve spiritual freedom.

So we see that both perspectives highlight a disdain for materialism, urging followers to seek higher spiritual values over worldly gains. This focus encourages a life centered on spiritual growth and ethical living.

Jesus is portrayed as the Savior who offers redemption and salvation through his teachings, life, death, and resurrection. His role as a redeemer is central to Christian theology. Gnostics also had a concept of a redeemer figure, often depicted as a divine being who descends into the material world to bring knowledge and liberation to trapped souls. In some Gnostic texts, Jesus is seen as this figure who imparts secret wisdom to select followers. The idea of a savior who provides a path to liberation is common to both Jesus' teachings and Gnostic thought, though the nature of salvation and the means of achieving it may differ.

Jesus frequently used parables and allegories to convey deeper spiritual truths, challenging listeners to look beyond literal interpretations and seek underlying meanings. Gnostic texts are rich with symbolic and allegorical language, designed to communicate complex spiritual concepts that require intuitive understanding and contemplation. Both approaches encourage followers to engage with teachings on a deeper, more intuitive level, fostering a mystical understanding of spiritual realities.

The concept of being "born again" is a central theme in Jesus' teachings, such as in **John 3:3-7** where he says, "*Truly, truly, I say to you, **unless one is born again he cannot see the kingdom of God***", and "*Truly, truly, I say to you, **unless one is born** of water and **the Spirit**, he **cannot enter the kingdom of God**.*" Thus, Jesus was emphasizing the need for a transformative spiritual rebirth to enter the kingdom of God. Gnostics also emphasized spiritual rebirth, viewing it as an awakening to one's true divine nature and the beginning of a journey toward spiritual enlightenment. The idea of rebirth underscores the transformative journey from ignorance to spiritual awareness, a shared theme that highlights the importance of personal evolution and awakening[51].

While there are similarities, significant differences exist as well. Jesus emphasized faith, love, and repentance, while Gnosticism often focused on esoteric knowledge and dualistic cosmology. However, some Gnostic sects viewed Jesus as a divine messenger who imparted secret teachings to his disciples. The *Gospel of Thomas*, a Gnostic text, includes sayings of Jesus that align with Gnostic thought.

The Essenes - Jesus and John the Baptist

The Essenes, a mystical Jewish sect that flourished during the Second Temple period, represent a profound spiritual movement distinct from the Pharisees and Sadducees, the other prominent Jewish groups of the time. Known for their ascetic practices, reverence for life, and esoteric teachings, the Essenes provide a lens through which the life and teachings of Jesus, as well as his cousin John the Baptist, can be more deeply understood. Their beliefs, practices, and eventual destruction by the Romans in 68 AD reveal a compelling narrative of spiritual resistance and enduring wisdom.

The Essenes lived in tight-knit communities, often in isolation from mainstream Jewish society. Their communal lifestyle emphasized simplicity, celibacy, and shared ownership of property, creating an environment free from the material corruption they saw in the world. Purity was central to their philosophy; they engaged in regular ritual bathing akin to baptism to maintain spiritual cleanliness. These practices reflected their quest for inner spiritual enlightenment, a personal journey toward divine mysteries that mirrored later gnostic traditions. The Essenes produced significant spiritual writings, such as the *Manual of Discipline* and the *War Scroll*, which emphasized the inner spiritual life, cosmic dualism, and a direct relationship with God.

Two notable Essene sects are often identified: the **Nazarenes** and the **Therapeutae**. The Nazarenes, sometimes associated with Jesus due

---

[51] Elaine Pagels, *The Gnostic Gospels* (New York: Random House, 1979), 121–125.

to his title "the Nazarene,"[52] and the Therapeutae, an Egyptian sect described by Philo of Alexandria, shared a commitment to healing and spiritual purification. The Therapeutae, located near Alexandria in Egypt, lived a life of simplicity, strict vegetarianism, and spiritual devotion. Their practices and beliefs strongly paralleled those of the Essenes in Judea, and it is probable that during their exile in Egypt, Joseph and Mary sought refuge among this community. Such an environment would have profoundly influenced the young Jesus, shaping his later emphasis on compassion, healing, and esoteric wisdom.

A growing body of belief also points to John the Baptist as a practicing Essene. John's ministry of baptism by water closely mirrors the Essenes' ritualistic bathing practices, which were not only acts of physical cleansing but also symbolic of spiritual purification and renewal. Living in the wilderness, John embraced an ascetic lifestyle that paralleled the Essenes' emphasis on simplicity and detachment from worldly distractions. The Gospels describe his diet as consisting of locusts and wild honey. Many scholars suggest that the reference to "locusts" may not signify insects but rather the fruit pods of the **carob tree**, also known as the "locust tree." This interpretation aligns with the Essenes' vegetarian practices and their reverence for life, rejecting the notion of consuming living creatures. Such dietary choices reinforce the alignment between John's lifestyle and the Essenes' beliefs.

The Essenes' divergence from the Pharisees and Sadducees was striking. While the Pharisees sought to interpret and apply both written and oral Torah to everyday life, and the Sadducees controlled the priesthood and centered their religious practices on the Temple's sacrificial system, the Essenes rejected both the oral traditions and the slaughter of animals. Their vegetarian lifestyle reflected their reverence for life, and they viewed the mass sacrifice of animals, such as the estimated 240,000 lambs killed in a single day during Passover, as a desecration of divine law. For the Essenes, the Temple's sacrificial system epitomized the corruption of institutionalized religion, a view

---

[52] Geza Vermes, *The Complete Dead Sea Scrolls in English* (London: Penguin Books, 1997), 42–45.

shared by Jesus when he overturned the money changers' tables and released animals destined for sacrifice. Declaring in **Matthew 21:13**, "*My house will be called a house of prayer, but you are making it a den of thieves!*", Jesus echoed the Essene critique of the Temple's commercialization and ritual excess.

The teachings of Jesus bear numerous parallels to Essene ideals. His emphasis on inner purity resonates with their rituals of spiritual cleanliness. His counsel to let one's "Yes" be "Yes" and "No" be "No" aligns with the Essene aversion to oath-taking, valuing truthfulness over formality. Jesus's ministry, centered on healing and compassion, mirrors the practices of both the Essenes and Therapeutae, who were renowned for their healing abilities. The Essenes' dualistic worldview, seeing life as a cosmic struggle between light and darkness, good and evil, aligns with Jesus's teachings on the Kingdom of God and the transformative power of spiritual enlightenment. His statement in the **Gospel of Thomas**, "*The Kingdom of God is **within you**,*" reflects the Essene and Gnostic emphasis on inner spiritual discovery.

The Essenes' tragic end came during the First Jewish–Roman War (66–73 AD). In 68 AD, Roman forces led by Vespasian destroyed Qumran, their settlement near the Dead Sea. Archaeological evidence of burned structures and abandoned manuscripts points to the community's violent demise. Anticipating the assault, the Essenes hid their sacred texts in nearby caves, preserving their teachings for future generations. These documents, now known as the **Dead Sea Scrolls**, offer invaluable insights into their beliefs and practices, bridging the gap between their world and ours.

The similarities between the teachings and practices of John and Jesus to the Essenes are too significant to ignore. John's emphasis on baptism, his ascetic lifestyle, and his possible vegetarian diet align strongly with Essene values. Similarly, Jesus's rejection of the Temple's sacrificial system, emphasis on spiritual purity, and focus on healing suggest he was influenced by their traditions. Whether they were formally trained by the Essenes or independently shared their values, their messages reflect the Essenes' ethos of compassion, mysticism, and a rejection of corruption. It is for these reasons that I personally believe that both John and Jesus were practicing Nazarene-Essene masters.

The story of the Essenes, their beliefs, and their ultimate destruction by the Romans adds depth to understanding Jesus's life and mission. Their devotion to inner spiritual knowledge, their rejection of institutionalized corruption, and their reverence for all life resonate through the teachings of Jesus and John the Baptist. By challenging the religious orthodoxy of their time, they embodied the Essene ideal of a life dedicated to God, purity, and the sacredness of creation. This legacy highlights the enduring influence of the Essenes on the spiritual evolution of humanity, as well as future Christian-Gnostic beliefs.

The actions and teachings of both Jesus and John reveal their deep alignment with the Essene worldview, especially their rejection of outward ritual in favor of inner transformation. But nowhere was this more powerfully demonstrated than in one of the most dramatic events of Jesus' ministry: His confrontation with the Temple system itself.

The End of Sacrifice: A Final Act of Mercy

One of the most profound insights about the life of Christ came to me recently, shedding new light on an age-old question: Why did Jesus willingly go to the cross? Beyond the layers of doctrinal interpretations, something deeper emerges when viewed through the Essene lens.

Jesus and his cousin John the Baptist were Essene masters who fundamentally rejected the bloody sacrificial system endorsed by the Sadducees and Pharisees. They viewed such practices as a distortion of true spirituality. The Temple had become not a house of prayer, but a slaughterhouse for profit. Historical records from the time, such as those of Flavius Josephus, estimate that over 250,000 lambs were sacrificed during a single Passover in Jerusalem. The blood of these animals was so excessive that stone troughs had been carved into the temple floor to carry it away.[53]

---

[53] Flavius Josephus, *The Jewish War*, Book 6, Chapter 9, Section 3.

When Jesus entered the Temple and overturned the money changers' tables, he was doing far more than protesting commerce. He was confronting an entire system of blood ritual, greed, and spiritual hypocrisy. Imagine the scene: the smell of blood hanging thick in the air, the bleating of terrified animals echoing off the stone walls, the chaos of bartering merchants, and the cries of those exchanging money, all in the supposed "House of God." Jesus, filled with righteous fury and sorrow, stormed in and physically overturned the tables, driving out the merchants and those selling sacrificial animals. With a whip of cords, he drove them all out of the temple courts, shouting, "My house shall be called a house of prayer for all nations, but you have made it a den of thieves!" He released the doves being sold in cages, setting free the very symbols of peace that had been imprisoned for profit.[54]

And then he did something even more radical: he willingly became the final sacrifice. Not because God demanded it, but because he knew that his death would end the need for all others.

His crucifixion was a symbolic and spiritual act meant to replace the ongoing slaughter of innocent animals. By offering himself, Jesus dismantled the legitimacy of temple sacrifice once and for all. As he said, quoting Hosea 6:6, "I desire mercy, not sacrifice." His death didn't endorse sacrifice. It ended it.

In that moment, Christ became the bridge between the old world of blood and the new path of compassion. He was not appeasing a wrathful God; he was breaking humanity free from a false understanding of God. This reframes the crucifixion, not as divine wrath satisfied, but as divine love revealed. And this is the very essence of Christ Consciousness: the realization that the Divine does not require suffering, but invites us into transformation through love, mercy, and the awakening of the inner Spirit.

---

[54] John 2:16; Matthew 21:12; Mark 11:15; Luke 19:45 – The synoptic gospels and John describe Jesus' cleansing of the temple. John explicitly mentions Jesus telling those who sold doves to take them away.

The Ebionites: Guardians of the Original Teachings[55]

I wish to begin this section by giving credit to Aron Abke, and his research team at 4D University, for much of the roots of the content in this section, much of which was originally derived from presentations in his course "*The Gospell Conspiracy*" at 4DUniversity.com. If you would like to take a deeper look into the information on the Ebionites, then I would highly recommend you check out his website, and his many videos available on YouTube.

The discovery of the Dead Sea Scrolls in the mid-20th century stands as one of the most significant archaeological finds of modern times. Unearthed between 1947 and 1956 in caves near Qumran along the Dead Sea's northwestern shore, these ancient manuscripts date from the third century BC to the first century AD. They include the oldest known surviving copies of the Hebrew Bible and a wealth of other Jewish writings, offering profound insights into the religious landscape during the Second Temple period.

The timing of this discovery is often viewed as divinely orchestrated. Emerging shortly before the establishment of the State of Israel in 1948, the scrolls provided tangible connections to ancient Jewish heritage at a pivotal moment in modern history. Their unearthing coincided with a period of renewed interest in biblical archaeology, enabling scholars to reassess and deepen their understanding of early Judaism and the early Christian movement.

However, the dissemination of the Dead Sea Scrolls was not immediate. After their discovery, access to the scrolls was limited to only high-level persons at the Vatican, leading to various speculations and theories about their contents. Some suggested that the Vatican was suppressing the scrolls due to potential challenges they might pose to established Christian doctrines. It wasn't until the early 1990s,

---

[55] Much of the roots of the content in this section was originally derived from Aron Abke's presentations in his course *The Gospell Conspiracy* at 4duniversity.com, 2024

over 40 years after their initial discovery, that the majority of the texts were made accessible to the scholarly community and the public. This delay hindered comprehensive research and fueled numerous conspiracy theories.

Catholic scholars insisted for forty years that the scrolls were works of the Essenes in the 3rd century BC, and they were written long before the time of Jesus. While some of the scrolls were certainly from this earlier incarnation of the Jewish Essene sect, many were actually written by a later evolution of the group calling themselves "the Ebion", which means "The Poor." This is thought to be a reference to the sermon on the mount in chapter-5 of Matthew when Jesus said, *"Blessed are the **poor in spirit**, for theirs is the **Kingdom of heaven**."* Gerhard Uhlhorn, a 19th-century theologian and historian, posited that the term "Ebionites" originally held a broader meaning, similar to the designation "Nazarenes," which was used as a general label for early followers of Christ. This group was also known as the "Followers of **The Way**."

The eventual release of the Dead Sea Scrolls has been instrumental in shedding light on the diversity of Jewish thought during the time of Jesus and has provided invaluable context for understanding the origins of Christianity. For those seeking a more authentic grasp of Christ's teachings, the scrolls offer a window into the beliefs and practices of groups like the Essenes, who emphasized communal living, asceticism, and a strict interpretation of Jewish law, which are all elements that resonate with the teachings of Jesus and his early followers. Thus, the Dead Sea Scrolls serve as a bridge to the past, illuminating the rich tapestry of religious thought from which Christianity emerged. Their discovery, though initially shrouded in controversy and delay, ultimately contributes to a more nuanced and profound understanding of Jesus's message and the early Christian community.

These scrolls, written between the third century BC and the first century AD, include sectarian writings, commentaries on Hebrew scriptures, and community rules. Among the key texts found in the Dead Sea Scrolls are the **Damascus Document**, **Habakkuk Pesher**,

Manual of Discipline, ***Temple Scroll***, and others that reveal a group deeply devoted to Mosaic Law and opposed to those who deviated from its teachings. Figures such as the "Teacher of Righteousness," the "Wicked Priest," and the "Spouter of Lies" reflect ideological battles within this community. Scholars like Robert Eisenman have posited that these figures correspond to James the Just (brother of Jesus), Ananias the High Priest, and Paul the Apostle, respectively. These writings, along with references by early church fathers, provide crucial insight into the beliefs of the Ebionites, a group that may have preserved the most authentic understanding of Jesus' teachings.

The Ebionites emerged as a direct continuation of the Jesus movement. Rooted in the Nazarene-Essene tradition, they adhered strictly to Mosaic Law, rejected Pauline doctrine, and upheld Jesus' role as a human Messiah chosen by God. Their theology and practices serve as a counterpoint to the Pauline Christianity that later gained dominance, offering a glimpse into the earliest form of Jesus' teachings.

There are some definite connections between the Qumran Ebionites and the 1st Century Christians as identified by correlations found within the writings of the two groups. For instance, **Acts 2:42-47** describes how the early followers of the apostles, "**had everything in common**. They **sold property and possessions** to give to anyone who had need", and they "**broke bread** in their homes and **ate together**". As for the Ebionites, **Community Rule 1** was "*All shall bring their knowledge and **possessions into the Community**. They shall **eat in common** and pray in common… the new adherents **property now concerns the congregation of the Poor**.*"

In **Matthew 5:3** Jesus states, "*Blessed are the **poor in spirit**, for theirs is the Kingdom of heaven*", and in the **War Scroll XIV** it says, "*The **poor in spirit** possess a power*". Then in **Matthew 5:5** Jesus says, "***Blessed are the meek**, for they **shall inherit the earth***", and in **Psalm 37 Pesher** it states, "*but **the meek shall possess the earth**".* Finally, in **Matthew 5:48** Jesus says, "*You must **therefore be perfect** as your **heavenly Father is perfect**"*, and in Community Rule VIII it says, "*those who walk **in the way of perfection** as commanded **by God**.*" Based on the book of Acts, we know that the original **twelve apostles** were the leadership of the early Christian church, and they were led by **James**, **Peter**, and **John**. According to the Community Rule, the group at Qumran was governed by a "**Council of 12**", of which **three** are "priests".

In **Matthew 5:17-20** Jesus says, "*I have not come to abolish the Law but to fulfill them…**not an iota, not a dot, will pass from the Law**…therefore whoever relaxes one of the least of these commandments and teaches others to do the same will be called the least in the kingdom.*" In the **Community Rule II** document it is stated, "*Anyone that transgresses **one word of the Law** of Moses, **on any point whatsoever**, shall be expelled, that the Law will endure for as long as the domain of Satan endures.*"

In **Matthew 5:33** it is stated, "***Thou shalt not forswear thyself**, but shalt perform unto the Lord thine **oaths**"*, and the Essenes refused to swear oaths altogether because they believed that a person's word should be trustworthy on its own. To them, taking an oath implied a lack of integrity and questioned the reliability of a person's statements without one. They considered speaking truthfully a sacred duty and felt that swearing by God's name might risk desecrating it if the oath were broken. Thus, they viewed oaths as unnecessary and potentially sinful.

In **Matthew 6:33** it says, "*But **seek ye first the kingdom of God**, and his righteousness; and all these things shall be added unto you.*" In the **Community Rule 1QS 1:1-3** is stated the following, "*They shall **seek God with all their heart and with all their soul**, and they shall do what is good and right before Him, as He commanded by the hand of Moses and all His servants the prophets. They shall love all that He has chosen and hate all that He has rejected.*" The Essenes prioritized living in harmony with God's will, believing that their lives should reflect divine righteousness. This parallels Jesus' emphasis on seeking the Kingdom of God, understood as alignment with divine order and justice.

Jesus instructs his followers in **Matthew 6** to, "*Lay not up for yourselves **treasures on earth** but lay up your **treasures in heaven**.*" **The Damascus Document (CD) VIII, lines 5-6** state, "*They **shall not desire silver or gold** or any of the wealth of the nations*". Additionally, the Community Rule highlights the importance of storing up good deeds and living in harmony with divine law, which aligns with the idea of laying up treasures in heaven when it states, "*Those who walk in the way of righteousness shall earn the **reward of eternal joy** and shall not perish with the riches of the nations or the pride of their hearts.*" This focus on spiritual wealth over material gain echoes Jesus' teachings in the Sermon on the Mount and suggests a commonality in worldview between the Essenes and Jesus' message in **Matthew 6**.

In **Matthew 23:9** Jesus commands his followers to, "***call no man your father*** *on earth, for you have **one Father, who is in heaven**.*" In this statement Jesus admonished his followers not to fall into the same patterns of pride, hierarchy, and self-exaltation that he saw in many religious leaders of his day. By emphasizing that God alone is the ultimate Father and source of authority, Jesus redirected focus away from earthly figures and toward divine sovereignty. In **Community Rule (1QS) V, lines 20-24** the Essenes state, "*They **shall not exalt themselves** above one another, but shall be humble, faithful, and just, acknowledging their transgressions and living together in unity under the **covenant of God**.*" Then in The Hymn of Thanksgiving (1QH) XVIII, lines 27-28 they say the following, "*You alone are **Father to all** the sons of Your truth and Master of all the hosts of **Your glory**.*"

Although in the New Testament writings the importance of James, the brother of Jesus, is seriously downplayed, it is clear from many sources that James was considered the most important of the original twelve apostles. In **The Gospel of Thomas saying 12** Jesus appoints James to be the leader of the disciples. In the **Ascents of James 8:20-21** it says that "***James the Just***" was ordained as bishop by Jesus. Then in the **Recognitions 4:35** it states, "*believe no teacher unless he bring from Jerusalem the testimonial of **James the Lord's brother***".

The **Didache**, or "*The Teaching of the **Twelve Apostles***," is a fascinating late first-century text that has long been recognized by scholars and theologians as a genuine artifact from the early Christian era. This document holds a unique place in Christian history, as it is believed to represent a manual of instruction on the teachings and practices of Jesus, conveyed directly by his disciples. Before the Council of Nicaea in 325 AD, the *Didache* was highly regarded among early Christian communities and may even have been considered part of the canon by some.

Unlike the epistles of Paul, the Didache is refreshingly straightforward in its approach. It eschews complex theological constructs in favor of simple, practical guidance rooted in the teachings of Jesus. The absence of Pauline theology is striking; there is no emphasis on justification by faith, the role of grace, or the abolition of the Mosaic Law. Instead, the Didache resonates with the tone of the Gospel accounts and shares much in common with the Epistle of James. Its core message revolves around repentance from sin, a wholehearted turning toward God, and living righteously by adhering to his commandments.

The Didache begins with an ethical section often referred to as "**The Two Ways**," outlining the **way of life** and the way of death. The way of life emphasizes loving God with all your heart and loving your neighbor as yourself, mirroring Jesus' teaching in the Gospels. It calls for humility, generosity, and non-retaliation, setting a standard for moral conduct that aligns closely with Jesus' Sermon on the Mount. The way of death, by contrast, describes behaviors and attitudes that lead to spiritual ruin, such as idolatry, murder, and greed. In **John 14:6** Jesus says, "*I am **the way**, the truth, and the **life**.*" In this verse Jesus is basically saying that he represents the "**way of life**" mentioned in the Didache.

The Didache also includes practical instructions for Christian practices such as baptism, fasting, prayer, and the Eucharist. Baptism, for instance, is prescribed to be performed in "living water" (flowing water), but allowances are made for pouring water over the head if immersion is not possible. The Lord's Prayer is presented as a model for daily prayer, to be recited three times a day, underscoring the importance of regular communion with God.

What makes the Didache especially compelling is its insight into the early Christian community's structure and priorities. It outlines guidelines for welcoming traveling apostles and prophets, emphasizing discernment to avoid exploitation by those who might abuse their position. It also provides instructions on appointing bishops and deacons, advocating for leaders who are humble and dedicated to serving others rather than seeking personal gain.

The simplicity and practicality of the Didache reflect the early church's focus on living out the teachings of Jesus in daily life. It stands as a powerful testament to the communal and ethical priorities of the first Christians, offering a window into a time when the faith was still closely tethered to its Jewish roots and free from the later doctrinal developments influenced by Greek thought and Roman authority. For modern readers, the Didache provides a refreshing return to the foundational principles of Christianity, echoing the clarity and urgency of Jesus' own words.

Paul's Struggles Against the Original Disciples

Saul of Tarsus was born a Jewish Pharisee and a Roman Citizen. He was a devout persecutor of the early Jewish Christians, who were called Nazarenes, Ebionites, and Followers of The Way. The tension between Paul and the original disciples James, Peter, and John is evident in the New Testament writings as well. In **Galatians 2:6-10**, Paul dismissively refers to the "***so-called pillars***" of the Jerusalem church, stating that, "*whatever they were **makes no difference to me***". In those days James, Peter and John were often referred to as the "Pillars of the Church." Thus, Paul is speaking about the three as if they mean nothing.

There were several early historians who drew this same conclusion about the Ebionites and their struggles with Paul over the true doctrine of Christ. Ambrosiaster, an anonymous Christian writer of the late 4th century (circa 366 AD), provides a significant early critique of groups like the Ebionites in his commentary on Paul's epistles. He noted that the Ebionites rejected the apostolic authority of Paul. This perspective aligns with the general view of the Ebionites as staunchly opposed to Paul's teachings, which they perceived as a departure from the original message of Jesus and the practices of the Jerusalem church led by the twelve apostles.

Irenaeus, an early Church Father writing around 180 AD, provides one of the earliest explicit mentions of the Ebionites' rejection of Paul. In his work *Against Heresies* (*Adversus Haereses*), Irenaeus describes the Ebionites as a Jewish-Christian sect that adhered strictly to the Mosaic Law and rejected Paul's teachings. He states that the Ebionites repudiated Paul, accusing him of being an apostate from the Law. Irenaeus's critique of the Ebionites reflects the theological conflicts that characterized early Christianity. As the movement expanded and diversified, groups like the Ebionites clung to their Jewish roots and resisted the theological innovations introduced by Paul, who sought to universalize Christianity by detaching it from Jewish legal obligations.

Eusebius of Caesarea, a 4th-century bishop and historian writing around 325 AD, which is notably the same year of the convening of the Council of Nicaea, also addressed the Ebionites and their rejection of Paul. In his seminal work *Ecclesiastical History* (*Historia Ecclesiastica*), Eusebius described the Ebionites as a heretical sect of Jewish Christians who adhered strictly to Mosaic Law. He noted that they rejected the epistles of Paul, considering him an apostate from the Law, and instead held to what they viewed as the unaltered teachings of Jesus and the apostles based in Jerusalem.

In **Acts 9:1-2** it says that, "*Saul was still breathing out **murderous threats** against the **Lord's disciples***", and that he was going to Damascus to look for men and women of "***The Way***", so that he could, "*take them as prisoners to Jerusalem.*" This is when Saul had his "conversion" on the road to Damascus, when he claimed he was confronted by the spirit of Christ. In this version of the experience Saul falls to the ground, and Jesus tells him to get up and enter the city. The travellers with Saul saw nothing, but heard a voice. Then in **Acts 22** Saul falls to the ground, and Jesus tells him to get up and enter the city. In this version, the travellers with Saul saw the light, but did not "understand" or "hear" the voice. Finally, in **Acts 26** Paul says that he and the travellers all saw the light and fell to the ground. Then Jesus gives Saul an elaborate appointment to preach the gospel to the gentiles. Intriguingly, Paul's story changes with each telling.

Paul's conflicts with the Jerusalem church culminated in **Acts 15**, where representatives of the church confronted him in Antioch over his teachings. The Jerusalem leadership stressed adherence to the Law and accused Paul of apostasy, reflecting the Ebionite critique that Paul had deviated from Jesus' teachings. This schism demonstrated the growing divide between Paul's theology and the Law-abiding message upheld by the original disciples. Later on in the same chapter there are a couple more mentions of some who, "*spoke evil of **The Way***", and "*there arose a great disturbance about **the Way***", both references to the Ebionites. Then in chapter 24 Paul, in order to get out of trouble, admits to being a "*follower of **the Way**, which they call a sect.*" Then in verse 22 we read that, "*Felix, who was well acquainted with **the Way***" decided to take over the case.

In the book of **2 Corinthians 11:1-5** Paul talks about the people being "*led astray*" by those that he calls the "***super-apostles***", or "***most eminent apostles***". It is apparent to anyone, with eyes to see, that Paul is referencing the original twelve apostles. Otherwise, why would he call them "***super-apostles***"? If he was truly speaking about anyone other than the original twelve, then he would have most certainly called them false apostles.

The Spouter of Lies and Paul's Gospel

The Dead Sea Scrolls describe figures such as the "*Spouter of Lies*" and the "*Man of Vanity*," who were seen as leading others away from the Law. For the Ebionites, these descriptions fit Paul, whose teachings replaced the covenant of works with a faith-alone doctrine. Paul's theology contradicted Jesus' explicit statements about the Law. Jesus declared in **Matthew 5:17-20**, "***Do not think that I have come to abolish the Law** or the Prophets; I have not come to abolish them but to **fulfill them**... whoever practices and teaches these commands* *will be called great in the kingdom of heaven."* By contrast, Paul wrote in **Romans 10:4**, "***Christ is the end of the law** so that there may be righteousness for everyone who believes."* This stark opposition revealed the divergence between Paul's teachings and Jesus' message, which the Ebionites sought to uphold.

Paul's writings often reflect an apparent egocentric focus, as seen in **Galatians 1:20**, where he insists, "*I am not lying*," and in **1 Corinthians 4:16**, where he exhorts, "*Therefore, I urge you, **be imitators of me**.*" Such statements stand in sharp contrast to Jesus' humility and servant leadership. Then when you read Paul's statements in **2 Corinthians 11**, it reads as though he was a master of conceit as he braggingly mentions "***boasting***" for a total of eight times. Then he brags about teaching the gospel to them "*free of charge*", and that he "*robbed other churches, taking wages from them to minister to you.*"

Then Paul goes on further in verses 23-27 to brag about how he has been more "*in labors*" and "*in stripes above measure*" than the said "***super-apostles***". As he elaborates that he has spent more time in prisons, been given 39 stripes a total of 5 times, been beaten with rods 3 times, stoned once, shipwrecked 3 times, spent a day and night "*in perils of waters*", he's been "*in perils of false brethren*", "*in weariness and toil, in sleeplessness often, in hunger and thirst, in fastings often, in cold and nakedness*". Does anyone with ears to hear actually believe all this? First of all, 39 lashes was considered all that the human body could withstand, and 40 was considered a death penalty. Christ was given 39 lashes during the crucifixion, so Paul here is saying that he endured three-times more than Jesus himself. Who actually survives a stoning, and what person is so cursed that they have been shipwrecked 3 times? This all sounds more akin to overblown ego than an honest report..

Crucially, **Paul never directly quotes Jesus** or references any of Jesus' teachings in his epistles. This absence is glaring, especially when compared to the other Gospels, which are filled with Jesus' words. Why then in the thirteen books of the New Testament commonly attributed to Paul did he never once directly quote any of

Jesus' actual teachings? How could a man who claimed that his gospel was superior to all others never actually discuss any of the teachings of the Master?

For example, in **Romans 2:16** Paul declared, "*God judges the secrets of men by **my gospel**.*" Then in **Romans 16:25** Paul says, "*to Him who is able to establish you according to **my gospel***". Also in **2 Timothy 2:8** he says, "*that Jesus Christ...was raised from the dead according to **my gospel**".*

In **John 5:43** Jesus says, "*I have come **in My Father's name**, and you do not receive Me; if another comes **in his own name**, you will receive him.*" Paul frequently introduces himself explicitly by his own name in his letters or uses explicit personal pronouns, often to assert his authority or emphasize his role as an apostle. Below are examples of this:

Romans 1:1 - "***Paul**, a servant of Christ Jesus, called to be **an apostle**, set apart for the gospel of God...*"

Romans 11:13 - "*Now **I** am speaking to you Gentiles. Inasmuch then as **I** am **an apostle** to the Gentiles, **I** magnify **my** ministry...*"

Romans 15:15 - "*But on some points **I** have written to you very boldly by way of reminder, because of the grace given **me** by God...*"

1 Corinthians 1:1 - "***Paul**, called by the will of God to be **an apostle** of Christ Jesus, and our brother Sosthenes...*"

1 Corinthians 3:4-5 - "*For when one says, 'I follow **Paul**,' and another, 'I follow Apollos,' are you not being merely human?*"

1 Corinthians 4:15-16 - "*For though you have countless guides in Christ, you do not have many fathers. For **I** became **your father** in Christ Jesus through the gospel. **I** urge you, then, **be imitators of me**.*"

1 Corinthians 16:21 - "***I, Paul**, write this greeting with **my** own hand.*"

2 Corinthians 1:1 - "**Paul, an apostle** of Christ Jesus by the will of God..."

2 Corinthians 10:1 - "*I, Paul, myself entreat you, by the meekness and gentleness of Christ—I who am humble when face to face with you, but bold toward you when I am away!*"

2 Corinthians 12:7 - "*...a thorn was given me in the flesh, a messenger of Satan to harass me, to keep me from becoming conceited.*"

Galatians 1:1 - "**Paul, an apostle**—not from men nor through man, but through Jesus Christ and God the Father, who raised him from the dead..."

Galatians 5:2 - "*Look: I, Paul, say to you that if you accept circumcision, Christ will be of no advantage to you.*"

Philippians 1:1 - "**Paul** and Timothy, servants of Christ Jesus, to all the saints in Christ Jesus who are at Philippi..."

Philippians 3:4-5 - "*Though I myself have reason for confidence in the flesh also. If anyone else thinks he has reason for confidence in the flesh, I have more...*"

1 Thessalonians 1:1 - "**Paul**, Silvanus, and Timothy, to the church of the Thessalonians in God the Father and the Lord Jesus Christ..."

1 Thessalonians 2:18 - "*...because we wanted to come to you—I, Paul, again and again—but Satan hindered us.*"

Philemon 1:1 - "**Paul**, a prisoner for Christ Jesus, and Timothy our brother..."

Philemon 1:9 - "*Yet for love's sake I prefer to appeal to you—I, Paul, an old man and now a prisoner also for Christ Jesus...*"

Philemon 1:19 - "*I, Paul, write this with my own hand: I will repay it— to say nothing of your owing me even your own self.*"

Based on the examples listed above, one could conclude that Paul was definitely coming "***in his own name***". While Paul mentions his own name and uses personal pronouns frequently in his epistles, Jesus, on the other hand, primarily uses personal pronouns to focus on his mission, identity, and relationship to the Father, often deflecting attention from himself to God. Yet Paul's apparent narcissism yields its ugly head even further in the passage below where he calls himself an "***angel of God***" and exalts himself to the level of Christ:

Galatians 4:11-14 - "*I am afraid of you, lest I have bestowed upon you labour in vain. Brethren, I beseech you, be as I am; for I am as ye are: ye have not injured me at all. Ye know how through infirmity of the flesh I preached the gospel unto you at the first. And my temptation which was in my flesh ye despised not, nor rejected; but received me as an angel of God, even as Christ Jesus.*"

In **Galatians 1:6-9** Paul basically extolls the people of the churches of Galatia for turning to "***another gospel***", which was the gospel taught by the original twelve apostles. Paul accuses the original apostles, calling them "***some that trouble you, and would pervert the gospel of Christ.***" Then Paul says, "*But even **if an angel from heaven** should preach to you a gospel contrary to the one we preached to you, **let him be accursed.**"* Then he ends with saying that the twelve apostles should "***be accursed.***"

In **Galatians 5:2-4** it reads, "*Indeed **I, Paul**, say to you that if you become circumcised, **Christ will profit you nothing**"* and "*You have become **estranged from Christ**, you who attempt to be justified by law; you have **fallen from grace**.*" Yet in **Acts 16:3**, Paul was taking on Timothy and, "***Paul** wanted to have him go on with **him**. And **he** took him and **circumcised him**"*. If Paul really felt this strongly about circumcision, then why would he force Timothy to be circumcised?

In **Acts 15:29** the original twelve disciples agreed to write a decree stating that gentiles did not have to follow the law to completeness, as long as they "**abstain from things offered to idols**, from **blood**, from *things strangled, and from sexual immorality.*" Yet, even with this huge concession, Paul still went on in **1 Corinthians 8:1-8** to tell the people, "*Therefore concerning the* **eating of things offered to idols**" it is okay to do. Thus, Paul once again goes against the directives of the original twelve apostles.

In **Romans 10:4** Paul states, "*For Christ is the* **end of the law**" and in **Galatians 3:13** Paul says, "*Christ hath redeemed us from the* **curse of the law**". Again in **Ephesians 2:15** Paul says that Christ was, "**abolishing the law** *of commandments*", and in **Romans 3:28** Paul says, "*For we maintain that a person is justified by faith* **apart from the works of the law**." Yet, as we have already seen in **Matthew 5:17-20** Jesus himself said, "**Do not think that I have come to abolish the Law** *or the Prophets;* **I have not come to abolish them but to fulfill them**… *whoever practices and teaches these commands will be called great in the kingdom of heaven.*" Again in **Matthew 5:18** Jesus states, "*For truly, I say to you, until heaven and earth pass away,* **not an iota, not a dot, will pass from the Law** *until all is accomplished.*" Once more in **Luke 10:25-29**, Jesus is asked, "*what must I do to inherit eternal life?*" Jesus instructs the man to **obey the Law**, and then he tells the parable of the Good Samaritan.

In **Galatians 2:16** Paul states, "*yet we know that a person* **is not justified by works of the law** *but through faith in Jesus Christ, so we also have believed in Christ Jesus, in order to be justified by faith in Christ and* **not by works of the law, because by works of the law no one will be justified**." Yet in **James 2:14-24** James asks, "*What doth it profit, my brethren, though a man say* **he hath faith,** *and* **have not works? can faith save him?**" and "*But wilt thou know,* **O vain man**, *that* **faith without works is dead**". In the statement of "**O vain man**", James was directly referencing Paul, the father of vanity. In contrast to Paul's gospel, in **Matthew 16:27** Jesus stressed the importance of works when he said, "*For the Son of Man is going to come…and then he will reward each person **according to what they have done**".

Then there are the writings in the Dead Sea Scrolls that reference these contrasting doctrines. In both the *Habbakuk Pesher* and the *Damascus* document "*the poor ones*" claim that the "**spouter of Lies**" seeks to have them all depart from the New Covenant and forsake the Law of Moses. The Ebionites have two manuscripts in the Dead Sea Scrolls, both of which are called "**Justification by Works**", which reaffirm their rejection of the position of "*cheap grace*" which the "**spouter of lies**" is teaching.

In the Habakkud Pesher it states, "*this concerns the **Spouter of Lies** who led many astray that he might build his **city of vanity with blood** and raise a congregation on **deceit**, causing many thereby to perform a service of vanity for the sake of its glory, and to be pregnant with works of deceit, **that their labour might be for nothing**.*"

To further expound upon the title of the "**Spouter of LIes**", let us consider Paul's own words on the matter. In **1 Corinthians 9:19-22** Paul is again bragging about himself, but this time he takes it to a whole new level by admitting that he is a chameleon. He says, "*unto the Jews **I became as a Jew***", and "*to them that are under the law, **as under the law**". However, when he is around the Gentiles he says, "*To them that are without law, **as without law**", and "*To the weak **became I as weak**", so that, "**I am made all things to all men**.*" Thus, we can safely assume that Paul was not a man of sincere authenticity by any measure.

In **2 Corinthians 12:16** Paul brags about being "**crafty**" when he says, "*Yet, **crafty** fellow that I am, I caught you by **trickery!**", and so he was bragging about his ability to deceive. Then in **2 Corinthians 11:1-3** Paul says, "*I hope you will **put up with me in a little foolishness**. Yes, please put up with me! **I am jealous for you** with a godly jealousy. I promised you to one husband, to Christ, so that **I might present you as a pure virgin to him**.*" Has anyone conceived of such coming from an individual who was hand-selected by Christ himself? He who has ears, let him hear…

It is obviously apparent that some people in Paul's day also caught on to the issues of honesty and integrity in Paul's words, because there are several instances where he has to actually state that he is not lying. In **2 Corinthians 11:31** Paul says, *"The God and Father of the Lord Jesus, who is to be praised forever, knows that **I am not lying**."* Then in **Galatians 1:20** Paul says, *"I assure you before God that what I am writing you **is no lie.**"* Again in **1 Timothy 2:7** he says, *"And for this purpose I was appointed a herald and an apostle—**I am telling the truth, I am not lying**—and a true and faithful teacher of the Gentiles."* Also in **Romans 9:1** Paul declares, *"**I speak the truth** in Christ—**I am not lying**"*.

However, in **Romas 3:7-8** Paul takes it to another level when he says, *"Someone might argue, '**If my falsehood enhances God's truthfulness and so increases his glory**, why am I still condemned as a sinner?' Why not say—**as some slanderously claim that we say**—Let us do evil that good may result?"* In this statement Paul is verifying in his own words that he has been accused of this very thing. Then in **Philippians 1:15-18** Paul says, *"It is true that **some preach Christ out of envy and rivalry**, but others out of goodwill. The latter do so out of love, knowing that **I am put here** for the defense of the gospel. The former preach Christ out of selfish ambition, not sincerely, supposing that **they can stir up trouble for me** while I am in chains. But what does it matter? The important thing is that in every way, **whether from false motives or true**, Christ is preached."* This appears to be an example of Paul projecting his traits onto his opponents.

In **Acts 23**, when Paul is brought before the Sanhedrin, he calls the high Priest Ananias a *"whitewashed wall"* and accosts him. This is when the people standing next to Paul say, *"How dare you insult God's high priest!"* At this point Paul realizes that his arrogance has gotten the best of him, so he says, *"Brothers, I did not realize that he was the high priest;"* Paul was born a Pharisee so he most certainly knew exactly who he was standing before. This was simply another example of Paul lying in an attempt to get out of trouble. Then in verses 6-10 Paul pits the Pharisees against the Sadducees in order to cause dissension between them.

The Ebionites maintained that Paul was not meeting with Jesus in secret, but with an evil spirit posing as Jesus to deceive him. They believed this was done to distort and corrupt the gospel of Jesus. In the following passage from **2 Corinthians** Paul himself admits that he was "*tormented*" **by a demon**, when he says God allowed, "*a messenger of Satan to torment me*" to keep him from being conceited. However, read the full passage below and understand that this is Paul admitting in his own words that he had demonic issues.

2 Corinthians 12:6-9 - "*Even **if I should choose to boast**, I would not be a fool, because **I would be speaking the truth**. But I refrain, so no one will think more of me than is warranted by what I do or say, or because of these **surpassingly great revelations**. Therefore, in order to keep me from becoming conceited, **I was given a thorn in my flesh, a messenger of Satan, to torment me**. Three times **I pleaded with the Lord to take it away from me**. But he said to me, 'My grace is sufficient for you, for my power is made perfect in weakness.' Therefore **I will boast** all the more gladly about my weaknesses, so that **Christ's power may rest on me**.*"

Then in **Romans 7:19-25** Paul talks about the "***sin that dwells in me***", and the "***evil is present with me***". Then he talks about his mind "*bringing me into captivity to **the law of sin which is in my members**.*" He ends with, "*So then, with the mind I myself serve the Law of God, but **with the flesh the law of sin**.*"

My question to you is this: If Jesus and his disciples were able to cast out demons left and right in the New Testament gospels, then why would God allow Paul to be tormented by a demon? Paul contends it is, "*in order to keep me from **becoming conceited**"*, but that seems a rather minuscule justification to allow demonic torment upon one of God's most valuable apostles. Would it not be in God's best interest to use another means of controlling Paul's arrogance than to have him be under demonic oppression? This would seem to me to suggest that God would have to be less than omnipotent in such a case. That is, of course, if Paul really was Christ's right-hand man.

In the late 1990s, through what felt like happenstance, I came into possession of a copy of Hyam Maccoby's provocative book, *The Mythmaker: Paul and the Invention of Christianity*[56]. At the time, I dismissed it as heretical without much consideration, and though I never read it fully back then, I now find it deeply ironic that this book crossed my path. Maccoby's arguments, which I once rejected outright, have since become relevant as I continue to explore the foundational questions surrounding Paul's role in shaping early Christianity.

Hyam Maccoby, a Jewish scholar and historian, was known for his critical perspectives on the New Testament and early Christian theology. In *The Mythmaker*, Maccoby presents a controversial thesis that challenges traditional understandings of Paul's vision and apostleship. He argues that Paul's experience on the road to Damascus may not have been an encounter with the risen Christ at all but possibly a visitation by a demonic entity. This startling claim is rooted in Paul's own writings, and the inconsistencies between his teachings and those of the original apostles.

One of Maccoby's key arguments centers around Paul's "*thorn in the flesh*," mentioned in **2 Corinthians 12:7**, which we already discussed above, "*Therefore, to keep me from being too elated, a thorn was given me in the flesh, **a messenger of Satan** to harass me, to **keep me from being conceited**.*" Maccoby interprets this passage as evidence that Paul was tormented by a demonic presence, which casts doubt on the spiritual origin of his revelations. Rather than viewing Paul's visions as divinely inspired, Maccoby suggests they may have been influenced by external forces that were not aligned with God's will.

---

[56] Hyam Maccoby, *The Mythmaker: Paul and the Invention of Christianity* (San Francisco: Harper & Row, 1986).

The Pseudo-Clementine Homilies, a collection of early Christian writings often associated with Ebionite thought, take this critique even further. These texts describe a series of debates between Peter and Simon Magus, a figure portrayed as a false prophet and heretic. Some scholars have suggested that Simon Magus may serve as a polemical stand-in for Paul, given their striking similarities in theological positions and claimed spiritual experiences. This interpretation is supported by Peter's arguments in the Homilies, which echo the critiques leveled at Paul by the Ebionites.

In **Homilies 17.19**, Peter directly challenges Simon Magus, saying: "*If our Jesus appeared to you in a vision, made himself known to you, and spoke to you, it was as someone who is angry with an adversary. But can anyone be made wise to teach through a vision? And if you say, 'It is possible,' then* **why did our teacher remain and converse with those who were awake for a whole year to instruct them? And how can we believe your story, that he appeared to you?** *And how were you alone deemed worthy to hear him?*" This passage casts doubt on the legitimacy of Simon Magus', or Paul's, claimed vision, emphasizing the importance of direct instruction from Jesus as experienced by the original apostles.

Peter goes on to warn about the dangers of deceptive spiritual experiences in **Homilies 17.12** when he says, "*For the Deceiver sends many false visions, so that he may lead astray those who follow such things, and turn them from the faith. But* **do not listen to any teacher unless he speaks the truth and proves it from our traditions**." This statement reflects the Ebionite skepticism toward Paul's claim that his gospel came through direct revelation, as declared by Paul in **Galatians 1:12**.

In **Homilies 2.17-18**, Peter critiques Simon Magus' reliance on visions, saying: "*For he who wants to persuade you of something must establish it by way of witnesses who have known the truth from the beginning and have walked with the Master...* **Do not accept teachings from those who claim authority based on visions or apparitions.**" Here, Peter underscores the value of apostolic tradition and direct witness over solitary spiritual experiences, a clear contrast to Paul's emphasis on his personal revelations.

The parallels between Simon Magus and Paul are difficult to ignore. Both figures claim authority based on supernatural revelation, both challenge the authority of the Jerusalem apostles, and both promote teachings that diverge from Jewish-Christian norms. For the Ebionites, these similarities likely reinforced their belief that Paul's visions were not of divine origin but rather the result of deception by an evil spirit.

Maccoby's critique extends to the theological framework that Paul established, which emphasized salvation through faith alone and minimized the role of the Mosaic Law. This, he argues, was a radical departure from the teachings of Jesus and the practices upheld by the Jerusalem Church under the leadership of James. The result, according to Maccoby, was a distortion of the original faith, with Paul's theology becoming the foundation for what would later be institutionalized as Christianity.

Though Maccoby's work is not widely accepted in mainstream Christian scholarship, it has contributed significantly to ongoing debates about Paul's role in early Christianity. The Pseudo-Clementine Homilies, whether taken literally or as allegorical critiques, offer a compelling lens through which to examine the tensions between the original apostles and Paul. For those exploring alternative interpretations of the New Testament, Maccoby's perspective and the Homilies provide provocative insights into the origins of the faith.

Paul's Troubles in Ephesus

Paul's experience in Ephesus reveals significant tension between his teachings and both the Jewish and Christian communities of the time. The accounts in Acts and Paul's letters suggest that his ministry in Ephesus, a major city in Asia Minor, was fraught with conflict, controversy, and outright rejection by many. These events offer a window into how Paul was perceived and why his teachings were often considered heretical or divisive.

Paul begins his letter to the **Ephesians 1:1** by asserting his divine calling when he declares, "*From **Paul, chosen by God to be an apostle** of Christ Jesus, to God's people who live in Ephesus...*" This salutation emphasizes Paul's self-proclaimed authority as an apostle, a title that was contested throughout his ministry. Despite his efforts to establish and guide the Ephesian church, Paul's relationship with the community in Asia appears to have deteriorated significantly over time. In **2 Timothy 1:15**, Paul laments, "*This you know, that **all those in Asia have turned away from me**.*" Given that Ephesus was a prominent city in Asia Minor and home to one of the seven churches addressed in Revelation, this statement underscores the widespread rejection Paul faced from the very communities he sought to lead.

Paul and his companion Luke both refer to a heresy trial in Ephesus. The nature of the accusations and the hostility toward Paul are described in **Acts 21:28**, where it says, "*The Jews from Asia, upon seeing him (Paul) in the temple, began to stir up all the crowd and laid hands on him, crying out, 'Men of Israel, come to our aid! **This is the man who preaches to men everywhere against our people and the Law**.*'" The charge that Paul was preaching against the Jewish people and the Mosaic Law mirrors the broader criticisms leveled against him by Jewish-Christian groups who remained faithful to the teachings of James and the Jerusalem Church. Paul's emphasis on liberty from the Law, as well as his outreach to Gentiles, placed him at odds with many within the Jewish-Christian community.

In **Acts 26:20-21**, Paul defends himself before King Agrippa, claiming, "*I kept declaring...that they should repent and turn to God, **performing works worthy of repentance**.*" This statement appears inconsistent with Paul's broader theology, as expressed in his epistles, which often deemphasize works in favor of faith. Critics argue that Paul's words here reflect a strategic attempt to align his message with more traditional Jewish-Christian teachings to avoid further persecution. His claim to have preached **repentance and works** contrasts sharply with accusations in **Acts 21:28** that he preached **against the Law**, raising questions about the consistency of his message, and the strength of his character.

The rejection of Paul by the churches in Asia, including Ephesus, is a critical point of contention in understanding his ministry. **Revelation 2:2** records Jesus' commendation of the Ephesian church for testing false apostles when he says, "***I know your works**, your toil and your patient endurance, and how you cannot bear with those who are evil, but **have tested those who call themselves apostles and are not**, and found them to be **false**.*" While Revelation does not explicitly name Paul, this passage has been interpreted by some as a critique of his apostleship, especially given the historical tensions between Paul and the Jewish-Christian communities in Asia Minor.

Paul's experiences in Ephesus illustrate the profound theological and cultural divisions within early Christianity. His teachings on the Law, Gentile inclusion, and justification by faith often clashed with the beliefs of Jewish-Christian groups who adhered to the Mosaic covenant. The heresy trial and subsequent rejection by the churches in Asia highlight the extent to which Paul's message was seen as divergent, if not outright heretical, by many of his contemporaries.

These events in Ephesus serve as a microcosm of the broader struggles within early Christianity to define orthodoxy and apostolic authority. For those examining the roots of Christian theology, Paul's contentious relationship with the Ephesian church raises important questions about the diversity of beliefs and practices in the first century.

Revelation's Theology: Aligning with Christ, Not Paul

The book of Revelation offers a striking perspective on early Christian theology, presenting themes and teachings that often stand in stark contrast to those of Paul. In particular, Revelation's focus on works, repentance, and adherence to specific commandments highlights tensions with Paul's emphasis on liberty in Christ and justification by faith. This divergence becomes especially apparent in passages addressing the consumption of meat sacrificed to idols, the emphasis on judgment according to works, and Jesus' critiques of lukewarm deeds.

One of the clearest points of contention between Revelation and Pauline theology is the issue of eating meat sacrificed to idols. In **Acts 15:20**, during the Jerusalem Council, James declares, "*...but we should write to them to **abstain from things polluted by idols**, from sexual immorality, from what has been strangled, **and from blood**.*" This directive, endorsed by the Jerusalem Church, explicitly forbids the practice of eating food associated with idol worship. It reflects a commitment to maintaining purity and avoiding any actions that could be construed as participation in idolatry.

However, Paul's teaching in **1 Corinthians 8:4-13** takes a permissive stance on this issue where he says, "*We know that an **idol is nothing** in the world, and that there is no God but one... But food does not bring us near to God; **we are no worse if we do not eat, and no better if we do**.*" Paul argues that eating meat sacrificed to idols is inconsequential for those who understand the spiritual emptiness of idols, provided it does not cause a weaker brother to stumble. This liberty-based approach contrasts sharply with the directive from James and the rebuke issued in Revelation.

In **Revelation 2:14**, Jesus admonishes the church at Pergamum when he says, "*But **I have a few things against you**: You have some there who hold to the teaching of Balaam, who taught Balak to put a stumbling block before the children of Israel, **so that they might eat food sacrificed to idols** and practice sexual immorality.*" Here, Jesus explicitly condemns the consumption of food sacrificed to idols, aligning with James' instruction and directly opposing Paul's permissive stance. By associating this behavior with Balaam's deceit, Revelation underscores the severity of the offense, framing it as a moral and spiritual failure.

Revelation repeatedly emphasizes that judgment is based on deeds, a theme that diverges from Paul's doctrine of justification by faith. In **Revelation 20:12**, the vision of the final judgment states, "*And I saw the dead, great and small, standing before the throne, and books were opened. Then another book was opened, which is the book of life. And **the dead were judged** by what was written in the books, **according to their deeds**.*"

Similarly, in **Revelation 22:12**, Jesus declares, "*Behold, I am coming soon, bringing my recompense with me,* **to repay each one for what he has done**." This consistent emphasis on works stands in contrast to Paul's writings, such as **Romans 3:28** when he says, "*For we hold that* **one is justified by faith apart from works of the law**." The emphasis in Revelation on works as the basis for judgment aligns more closely with the teachings of James, who writes in **James 2:17**, "*So also* **faith by itself, if it does not have works, is dead**."

In the message to the church in Laodicea, Jesus critiques their lukewarm works and calls for repentance when he says in **Revelation 3:15-16**, "***I know your works****: you are neither cold nor hot. Would that you were either cold or hot! So,* **because you are lukewarm**, *and neither hot nor cold,* **I will spit you out of my mouth**." He continues in **Revelation 3:19** by saying, "*Those whom I love, I reprove and discipline, so be zealous and* **repent**." This passage reinforces the importance of deeds and the necessity of repentance as expressions of genuine faith. While not a direct critique of Paul, it validates a theology that prioritizes actions over mere belief, which is a position that contrasts with Paul's writings, such as **Ephesians 2:8-9** where he says, "*For* **by grace you have been saved through faith**. *And this is not your own doing; it is the gift of God,* **not a result of works**, *so that no one may boast*."

In **Revelation 2:2**, Jesus commends the church at Ephesus for their discernment by saying, "***I know your works****, your toil and your patient endurance, and how you cannot bear with those who are evil, but* **have tested those who call themselves apostles and are not**, *and found them to be* **false**." This statement has led some to speculate that it could be a reference to Paul, and his troubles in Ephesus which we covered earlier.

Revelation presents a theology that emphasizes works, repentance, and adherence to specific commandments, standing in contrast to Pauline doctrines of liberty and justification by faith. The rebukes of practices like eating meat sacrificed to idols and the emphasis on judgment according to deeds align more closely with the teachings of James and the Jerusalem Church. Whether viewed as a direct critique or as a validation of non-Pauline theology, Revelation highlights the diversity of thought within early Christianity and challenges readers to reconsider the foundations of their faith.

The Roman Catholic Suppression of Ebionite Teachings

Paul's version of the gospel eventually won in the end because Rome was intensely anti-semitic. Constantine was looking for a way to centralize power in the heavily divided Roman Empire, and he did so via the Council of Nicaea in 325 AD.

The fact is that the original true gospel of Jesus Christ cannot be weaponized, because it is based on self-sacrifice in service to others, and unconditional Love towards all men. You cannot really maintain a powerful army based on the concept of turning the other cheek. However, Paul's gospel gave the Roman Catholic Church incredible power, especially when it comes to "heretics" and "holy wars". All the Church had to do was accuse someone of heresy for any number of reasons, and that gave them justification to take everything that person owned, and burn them at the stake. This concept simply expanded to entire groups of people and nations with the Holy Wars and the Inquisition.

The Roman Catholic Church's rise to power marked the systematic suppression of Ebionite teachings. By the fourth century, councils such as Laodicea in 364 AD and Rome in 382 AD declared Ebionite texts to be heretical. Possession of these writings was **punishable by death**, as evidenced by the decrees from Pope Damasus that banned alternative gospels and writings associated with the Nazarenes and Ebionites.

Decree of Council of Rome on the Biblical Canon:

*...and what also **all disciples** of heresy and of the heretics or schismatics, whose names we have scarcely preserved, have taught or compiled, we acknowledge is to be not merely rejected but excluded from the whole roman catholic and apostolic Church and with its*

authors and the adherents of its authors to be damned in the inextricable shackles of anathema for ever.

- *Itinerary (book of travels) under the name of the **apostle Peter**, which is called the Nine Books of the holy **Clement** apocryphal*
- *Acts under the name of the **apostle Andrew** apocryphal*
- *Acts under the name of the **apostle Thomas** apocryphal*
- *Acts under the name of the **apostle Peter** apocryphal*
- *Acts under the name of the **apostle Philip** apocryphal*
- *Gospel under the name of **Matthias** apocryphal*
- *Gospel under the name of **Barnabas** apocryphal*
- *Gospel under the name of **James** the Younger apocryphal*
- *Gospel under the name of the **apostle Peter** apocryphal*
- *Gospel under the name of **Thomas** apocryphal*

Imperial Rome beginning with Theodosius' reign 379-395 outlawed any religion but that of the "bishops of Rome" in Codex Theod. XVI, I, 2. If any heretical material was found, **the owner suffered the death penalty**. Just reflect on that for a moment… Even if you were a well-to-do nobleman of stature, with a large library of literature on your estate. If someone from "The Church" found even a single copy of just one of the Ebionite writings we have referenced in this book, then you could be killed, your library would most likely be burned, and your family could literally lose everything. These tactics were so effective that there is not a single record of any Ebionite writing that we can find preserved anywhere, in any library, other than perhaps the Vatican's private archives. What better way to ensure that no documents in opposition to the Church's stance would survive the test of time. Thus, leaving the Holy Roman Empire as the sole delegator of "God's will."

The Ebionites' struggle exemplifies the tension between institutionalized power and authentic spirituality. Their steadfast commitment to the teachings of Jesus, their rejection of Paul's deviations, and their persecution by the Roman Church echo the resistance of later movements like the Cathars, who also sought to preserve a purer Christianity. The Ebionites' legacy challenges readers to reexamine historical narratives and seek the truth behind the traditions they have inherited.

The Cathars vs. The Empire

The Cathars were a spiritual group that emerged in the 12th century who were primarily located in the Languedoc region of southern France. They represented a significant movement within medieval Christianity which advocated for a form of faith that diverged sharply from the Catholic Church's Empirical teachings. Their beliefs were rooted in a dualistic worldview where they saw the material world as flawed or evil. They believed that the physical plain was created by a lesser deity, while the spiritual realm was associated with a higher, good God. This perspective led them to embrace asceticism, and practice a life of simplicity and spiritual purity. Thus, the Cathars could be considered to be a medieval Gnostic sect, much like the Nazarene Essenes were in the time of Christ[57].

The Cathars rejected the Catholic sacraments, viewing them as corrupt and ineffective. They believed that the material world, including the Church and its rituals, was tainted by the evil god of the material realm. Specifically, they denied the validity of key sacraments such as the catholic baptism and communion, seeing them as instruments of control rather than true pathways to spiritual enlightenment. Instead, they practiced their own version of communion, focusing on personal spiritual experience (i.e. - Gnosis) and the inner transformation of the individual.

The Cathars attracted a significant following among the populace, appealing to those disillusioned with the corruption and materialism of the Roman Catholic Church. Their leaders, known as "perfects," embodied their ideals of holiness and spiritual discipline, serving as spiritual guides for their communities. However, as we have seen before it can be a dangerous thing to challenge the dogma of the Empire.

---

[57] Karen R. King, *The Gospel of Mary of Magdala: Jesus and the First Woman Apostle* (Santa Rosa, CA: Polebridge Press, 2003), 85–90.

The rise of the Cathars posed a direct threat to the authority of the Catholic Church, leading to intense conflict. In response, Pope Innocent III launched the Albigensian Crusade in 1209[58], aimed explicitly at eradicating the Cathar heresy. This brutal campaign was marked by violence and atrocities, as Crusaders swept through the region, targeting not just Cathars but also sympathizers among the local populace.

The siege of Béziers in 1209 is one of the most infamous events of the Crusade, where thousands of inhabitants, including many innocent bystanders, were killed. The response of the Crusaders to the question of how to distinguish between Catholics and Cathars was chillingly simple: "Kill them all; Let God sort them out." This exemplified the horrific violence that characterized the campaign[59].

As the crusade progressed, the Empirical Catholic Church established the Inquisition to root out remaining Cathar communities. The Inquisition employed methods of interrogation, torture, and execution to enforce conformity and punish dissent. Many Cathars were burned at the stake, while others were forced to recant their beliefs under extreme duress.

Despite the brutality of the Empirical Church's efforts, pockets of Cathar belief persisted for some time, but the movement ultimately declined under the relentless pressure of persecution. By the end of the 13th century the Cathars had been largely eradicated, their teachings and practices suppressed. Yet the Cathar legacy endures as a symbol of spiritual resistance against oppressive Empirical religious authority.

---

[58] Malcolm Barber, *The Cathars: The Most Successful Heresy of the Middle Ages* (Manchester: Manchester University Press, 1995), 78–83.
[59] Jonathan Riley-Smith, *The Crusades: A History* (New Haven: Yale University Press, 2005), 231–235.

Chapter-6: Others Similar to Jesus

Some suggest that the narrative of Jesus' life parallels myths associated with other spiritual leaders throughout history. Strikingly, there are many similarities between the stories in the life of Jesus as told in the New Testament and many others from the past. Let us examine a few of these other leaders.

Krishna - Circa 3228–3102 BC

Krishna, a central figure in Hinduism, is revered as an incarnation of the god Vishnu. His narrative features a miraculous birth, divine lineage, extraordinary deeds, and a mission to restore righteousness. His life story includes a miraculous birth, divine parentage, the performance of miracles, and a mission to rid the world of evil. Krishna was also a teacher of dharma (righteousness) and emphasized devotion, much like Jesus' teachings on love and faith.

The lives of Jesus and the great Hindu teacher Krishna share many striking similarities, revealing deep parallels across their spiritual narratives. Both were visited at birth by wise men guided by a star, signifying their divine purpose from the moment they entered the world. They were each referred to as the "Son of God" and considered the second person of the Holy Trinity within their respective traditions. Interestingly, both had earthly fathers who were carpenters, underscoring their humble beginnings.

Jesus and Krishna were both called "Savior" and claimed to embody the "Resurrection" of life, offering hope and renewal to their followers. Each endured extended fasting in the wilderness and taught the profound importance of forgiving one's enemies. They were renowned for their miracles, healing "all manner of diseases," casting out demons, and even raising the dead. Both were criticized for associating with "sinners," further emphasizing their teachings of compassion and inclusivity.

Symbolically, Jesus was known as the "Lion of the tribe of Judah," while Krishna was called the "Lion of the tribe of Saki," reflecting their shared strength and spiritual authority. Their stories also include descending into Hell, followed by resurrection and eventual ascension into Heaven. Even their names, Christ and Krishna, bear an uncanny resemblance, further highlighting the profound connection between their teachings and lives.

Krishna was born to Devaki and Vasudeva in a prison cell. His birth was foretold to his evil uncle, King Kamsa, who feared the prophecy that Devaki's eighth son would kill him. To prevent this, Kamsa killed all of Devaki's previous children, but Krishna was miraculously saved. This is somewhat similar to the story of King Herod in the New Testament, who sought to kill the newborn Jesus after hearing a prophecy about the coming of a new king. In some versions of the story, it is said that after Krishna's birth, divine beings and sages visited him to offer blessings and acknowledge his divine incarnation. These figures, much like the Magi in the story of Jesus, recognized Krishna's divine nature and his role in the cosmic order[60].

Krishna is considered an incarnation, or avatar of the god Vishnu, making him a divine figure born in human form. This parallels the concept of Jesus as the Son of God, born of the Virgin Mary. After his birth, Krishna was secretly taken across the Yamuna River to the village of Gokul to protect him from Kamsa's wrath. This mirrors the flight of the Holy Family to Egypt to protect Jesus from King Herod.

Krishna performed many miracles as a child, including lifting the massive Govardhan Hill to protect his village from torrential rains sent by the god Indra. These miracles are similar to the miracles Jesus performed, such as calming the storm and feeding the 5,000, and like Jesus, Krishna was known for his healing powers as well. In one story, he revived the dead son of his guru, Sandipani, mirroring Jesus' resurrection of Lazarus and others.

---

[60] R.C. Zaehner, *The Bhagavad Gita: With the Commentary of Sankara* (Oxford: Oxford University Press, 1986), 45–50.

Krishna's teachings are encapsulated in the Bhagavad Gita, where he expounds on dharma (duty/righteousness), karma (action), and bhakti (devotion). His teachings emphasize the importance of living a righteous life and being devoted to God, similar to Jesus' teachings about love, faith, and following God's will. He is often seen as a protector and savior of humanity, intervening in times of moral decline to restore dharma, akin to Jesus' role as the savior of mankind who came to earth to redeem humanity from sin[61].

Krishna's death is described in the Mahabharata and other Hindu texts. According to the story, after the great war of Mahabharata and the destruction of the Yadava dynasty, Krishna withdrew to the forest. While resting under a tree, he was accidentally struck by an arrow shot by a hunter named Jara, who mistook Krishna's partially visible foot for a deer. The arrow hit Krishna in his heel, which was his only vulnerable spot, much like Achilles' heel in Greek mythology. According to some versions of the story, the arrow that struck Krishna in the foot was embedded in the tree he was resting under. This has some similarity to the story of Jesus being nailed to the cross. After being struck by the arrow Krishna forgave the hunter and accepted his fate, recognizing it as the appropriate time for his departure from the earthly realm. Jesus also prayed, "Father, forgive them for they know not what they do." This event marks Krishna's exit from the world, known as his mahasamadhi.

After Krishna's departure, his teachings and stories were spread by his disciples, much like how Jesus' apostles spread Christianity after his resurrection. His life story is filled with symbolism that resonates with themes of divine love and sacrifice, similar to the Christian narrative of Jesus. He was one of the ten avatars of Vishnu who was believed to incarnate whenever there is a decline in righteousness. This concept of recurring divine intervention has some parallels with the Christian belief in the Second Coming of Christ.

---

[61] Eknath Easwaran, *The Bhagavad Gita: A New Translation* (Tomales, CA: Nilgiri Press, 2007), 57–61.

Zoroaster - Circa 1500–1000 BC

Zoroaster, also known as Zarathustra, was the founder of Zoroastrianism, which is one of the world's oldest monotheistic religions. There are several thematic and symbolic similarities between Zoroaster and Jesus, despite the differences in their cultural and religious contexts.

Zoroaster, also known as Zarathustra, was born during an era marked by widespread falsehoods and the worship of daevas, which were deities associated with chaos and destruction in Zoroastrianism. These evil forces, who were led by the spirit of destruction and chaos called Angra Mainyu, were aware of a prophecy that foretold the birth of a great prophet who would promote the worship of Ahura Mazda, and lead humanity away from their negative influence. Fearing the loss of their influence over humanity, they plotted to destroy the child at birth.

His mother, named Dughdova, was said to have conceived him after a divine event. This is often described as the light of the supreme god, Ahura Mazda, entering her womb. His birth, heralded by miraculous signs, was safeguarded against malevolent forces, drawing parallels to the early life of Jesus. The daevas attempted various methods to kill the infant Zoroaster. In one story they tried to send wolves to devour him, but the animals were either repelled or tamed by the divine aura surrounding the child. In another account, they tried to use fire to kill him, but Zoroaster remained unharmed, protected by Ahura Mazda's power. These two miracles are very reminiscent of the biblical stories of Daniel when he was cast into the lion's den found in **Daniel 6**, and the fiery furnace **Daniel 3**.

The daevas influenced evil humans, particularly the wicked priests and rulers who were loyal to the old ways of worshiping false gods and practicing corrupt rituals. This can be seen as similar to the Pharisees who sought to kill Jesus. These individuals, fearing the prophetic child, also sought to kill Zoroaster through various means, but all their attempts were thwarted by divine intervention[62].

Zoroaster is regarded as a prophet who received divine revelation from Ahura Mazda. He preached the importance of following the path of righteousness and rejecting the forces of evil. His teachings emphasized the importance of good thoughts, good words, and good deeds. Jesus is considered the Son of God and a prophet who taught the message of love, compassion, and righteousness. His teachings, such as those found in the Sermon on the Mount, emphasized the importance of faith, love, and moral behavior.

Zoroaster was tempted by the evil spirit Angra Mainyu who tried to lure him away from his mission. Zoroaster resisted these temptations, affirming his commitment to Ahura Mazda and the path of righteousness. Jesus was tempted by Satan in the wilderness after his baptism. Satan offered Jesus worldly power, tried to seduce him with food while he was fasting, and tested his faith. Jesus resisted all of these temptations, demonstrating his dedication to God's will.

Zoroaster taught that there would be a final judgment at the end of time, where all souls would be judged based on their deeds. The righteous would be rewarded with eternal life in paradise, while the wicked would be punished. This belief in a final judgment and the resurrection of the dead is central to Zoroastrian eschatology. Jesus also taught about a final judgment where all people would be judged based on their faith and actions. The righteous would be granted eternal life in heaven, while the wicked would face eternal punishment.

Zoroastrianism includes the belief in a future savior, known as the Saoshyant, who will be born of a virgin and will lead humanity in the final battle against evil, ultimately restoring righteousness and bringing about the final renovation of the world. In Christianity, Jesus is seen as the Messiah and the savior of humanity. The birth and life of Jesus can

---

[62] Mary Boyce, *Zoroastrians: Their Religious Beliefs and Practices* (London: Routledge & Kegan Paul, 1979), 51–55.

be potentially seen as the embodiment of the Zoroastrian future savior, the Saoshyant. Christians believe in the Second Coming of Christ, where Jesus will return to judge the living and the dead and establish a new heaven and a new earth[63].

Zoroaster is attributed with performing miracles, such as healing the sick and controlling natural elements. His miraculous acts were seen as signs of his divine connection and authority as a prophet. Jesus is renowned for performing numerous miracles, including healing the sick, walking on water, calming the storm, turning water into wine, and raising the dead. These miracles are central to his identity as the Son of God and savior.

Zoroaster introduced the concept of ethical monotheism, where the worship of one supreme god, Ahura Mazda, is intertwined with living a life of moral and ethical integrity. Zoroaster's teachings emphasized the importance of living according to the principles of truth, justice, and righteousness. Jesus's teachings also promote ethical monotheism, emphasizing the worship of one God and the importance of loving one's neighbor, acting justly, and living a life of righteousness. The greatest commandments, according to Jesus, are to love God and to love others.

Buddha - Circa 563–483 BC

Siddhartha Gautama, later venerated as the Buddha, was born to Queen Maya and King Suddhodana in Lumbini, Nepal, circa 563 BC. According to legend, Queen Maya experienced a visionary dream of a white elephant entering her side, heralding the arrival of an extraordinary being. Siddhartha was born under miraculous circumstances, with some texts describing his birth as painless and accompanied by heavenly signs. Similarly, Jesus was born to the Virgin Mary in Bethlehem, with divine proclamations marking the significance of his arrival. His birth was announced by angels and

---

[63] N.T. Wright, *Jesus and the Victory of God* (Minneapolis: Fortress Press, 1996), 390–395.

marked by the appearance of a star, which guided the Magi to his birthplace[64].

Before achieving enlightenment, Siddhartha faced profound trials from Mara, the embodiment of temptation, who sought to divert him from his meditative quest beneath the Bodhi tree. Mara sent his daughters to seduce him, his army to attack him, and finally, challenged his right to enlightenment. Siddhartha resisted all temptations and achieved enlightenment. Similarly, after his baptism, Jesus spent 40 days in the wilderness, where he was tempted by Satan. Satan offered him worldly power, tried to seduce him with food while fasting, and challenged his faith. Jesus resisted all of Satan's temptations, affirming his unwavering commitment to God's will. Just as Buddha attained enlightenment by resisting Mara's temptations, Jesus emerged from the wilderness fortified in spiritual resolve after overcoming Satan's trials[65]. With the divine anointing of the "Christ Consciousness," symbolized by the dove descending upon his Third Eye, Jesus was empowered to begin his ministry. This moment marked not only the end of his trial but the beginning of his divine mission to teach humanity, much like Buddha's path of enlightenment guided others to transcend suffering.

Buddha's teachings center on compassion, loving-kindness, and respect for all living beings, forming the cornerstone of his spiritual philosophy. He taught the Noble Eightfold Path as a guide to right living, which includes right speech, right action, and right livelihood. Jesus' teachings also emphasize love and compassion, particularly the commandment to "*love your neighbor as yourself*" and to "*love your enemies.*" The Sermon on the Mount encapsulates much of his ethical teachings, which include caring for the poor, being merciful, and striving for peace.

---

[64] Karen Armstrong, *Buddha* (New York: Penguin Books, 2001), 19–22; N.T. Wright.
[65] N.T. Wright, *Jesus and the Victory of God* (Minneapolis: Fortress Press, 1996), 340–345.

Following his enlightenment, Buddha formed a community of disciples, the Sangha, dedicating his life to guiding them and others on the path to spiritual awakening. His disciples were responsible for spreading his teachings across Asia, forming the foundation of Buddhism. Jesus also gathered a group of disciples, the twelve apostles, who followed him and learned from his teachings. After his crucifixion and resurrection, his disciples were tasked with spreading his message, leading to the formation of Christianity.

While Buddha's teachings emphasize self-effort and inner transformation, various accounts attribute miraculous acts to him, such as levitating, walking on water, multiplying his form, and calming wild animals. Jesus was renowned for performing many miracles, including healing the sick, walking on water, feeding thousands with a few loaves of bread and fish, and raising the dead.

Buddha emphasized the necessity of detachment from material wealth and desires, identifying them as the root of human suffering. He encouraged his followers to live a simple, mindful life focused on spiritual goals rather than worldly possessions. Jesus also warned against the dangers of material wealth, teaching that "*it is easier for a camel to go through the eye of a needle than for a rich man to enter the kingdom of God*." He advocated for a life of simplicity and spiritual richness over material abundance.

Buddha's teachings advocate for nonviolence in thought, word, and deed. He taught that hatred does not cease by hatred but by love, and he encouraged his followers to live peacefully with all beings. Jesus also preached nonviolence, advising his followers to "*turn the other cheek*" when struck and to live in peace with others. He is often referred to as the "Prince of Peace."

Siddhartha Gautama was born a prince and renounced his royal life in pursuit of spiritual enlightenment. He rejected the trappings of power, wealth, and luxury to seek a higher truth. Jesus, though seen by some as a potential political leader or king, rejected worldly power and focused on spiritual leadership. When offered earthly kingdoms by

Satan during his temptation, Jesus refused, emphasizing his kingdom was not of this world[66].

Buddha taught the importance of forgiveness and letting go of anger and resentment. He believed that holding onto anger was like grasping a hot coal with the intent of throwing it at someone else. The result is that you are the one who gets burned. Jesus also emphasized forgiveness, famously teaching his followers to forgive others "*seventy times seven*" times and to pray for those who persecute them.

These parallels underscore shared spiritual themes in the teachings of Buddha and Jesus, such as compassion, nonviolence, detachment from materialism, and the quest for spiritual enlightenment or salvation. Despite the differences in their cultural and religious contexts, their teachings continue to resonate with followers around the world.

The Law of One - 1981-1984

The *Law of One* material[67], also known as the *Ra Material*, is a series of channeled teachings that emerged from sessions conducted between 1981 and 1984 by a group of researchers: Don Elkins, Carla Rueckert, and Jim McCarty. At its core, the *Law of One* teaches that all of creation is unified, emanating from one infinite source, which they refer to as the "Infinite Creator." This source is the foundation of all existence, and every being is an expression of it. The teachings explore profound spiritual concepts, including the unity of all life, the evolutionary journey of consciousness, free will, the nature of love, and the process of spiritual awakening. The *Law of One* emphasizes living in alignment with love and understanding as pathways to transcend duality and recognize the inherent oneness of all things.

---

[66] Karen Armstrong, *Buddha* (New York: Penguin Books, 2001), 26–30; N.T. Wright, Jesus and the Victory of God (Minneapolis: Fortress Press, 1996), 355–360.
[67] Don Elkins, Carla Rueckert, and Jim McCarty, *The Ra Material: An Ancient Astronaut Speaks, 1st ed.* (Louisville, KY: Schiffer Publishing, 1984), 1-55.

The teachings of Jesus Christ often reveal a profound and universal truth, that all of creation is interconnected, forming a divine unity with the Creator at its center. This concept aligns with the "*Law of One*," as do many of the world's philosophies. For example, in Hinduism the concept of Brahman as the divine source from which all individual souls emerge and ultimately return reflects the unity of all existence. Similar concepts are found in the Buddhist Heart Sutra, the Taoist belief that "All things are one," the belief in Sufism that "all existence is ultimately one," the concept in Hermeticism of "As Above, So Below," and many Native American beliefs teach the unity and sacredness of all living things. This is a concept which also aligns with what Quantum Physics calls the Quantum Field, but this is a subject we will cover in-depth in a later book. The Law of One challenges dualistic thinking and encourages a holistic view of existence, where separation is an illusion, and unity is the ultimate reality.

In contrast, Pauline philosophy frequently emphasizes humanity's separation from God, portraying salvation as a transactional process requiring belief in Christ's sacrificial death. This dualistic framework stands in stark opposition to the message of oneness and divine immanence found in Jesus' teachings. As we explore the concepts of the Law of One, we will see how they resonate with the words of Jesus and simultaneously highlight contradictions within Pauline theology.

At the heart of the *Law of One* is the idea that all beings and creation are aspects of the One Infinite Creator, inherently unified. This principle is beautifully echoed in Jesus' prayer in **John 17:20-23**:

> "*I do not pray for these alone, but also for those who will believe in Me through their word; that **they all may be one**, as You, Father, are in Me, and I in You; that they also **may be one in Us**, that the world may believe that You sent Me. And the glory which You gave Me I have given them, that **they may be one just as We are one**: I in them, and You in Me; that **they may be made perfect in one**.*"

Here, Jesus explicitly calls for unity among His followers, a unity that mirrors His oneness with the Father. This vision of interconnectedness stands in stark contrast to Pauline theology, which often emphasizes humanity's fallen nature and separation from God. For example, as Paul writes in **Romans 3:23**, "*For **all have sinned** and fall short of the glory of God.*" Rather than affirming the inherent unity of humanity with the Divine, Paul's perspective perpetuates a sense of alienation that is inconsistent with Jesus' message.

The Law of One emphasizes **service to others** as the highest expression of divine unity. In this framework, serving others is equivalent to serving the Creator, as all are One. Jesus encapsulates this principle in **Matthew 25:40** when he says, "*Truly I say to you, whatever you did **for one of the least of these** brothers and sisters of mine, **you did for Me**.*" This teaching reflects the interconnectedness of all of humanity and the divine imperative to act with love and compassion.

In contrast, Pauline theology often prioritizes belief over action. In **Romans 10:9**, Paul asserts, "*If you **declare with your mouth**, 'Jesus is Lord,' and believe in your heart that God raised Him from the dead, you will be saved.*" While Paul does acknowledge the importance of love in passages like **1 Corinthians 13**, his overall emphasis on faith as the sole means of salvation shifts focus away from the active, loving service to others that Jesus was teaching.

A cornerstone of the Law of One is the understanding that the Divine resides within each individual. Jesus articulates this truth in **Luke 17:21** when he said, "*Nor will they say, 'See here!' or 'See there!' For indeed, **the kingdom of God is within you**.*" This statement invites individuals to look inward for divine connection, affirming that the presence of God is not external but intrinsic to all.

Conversely, Pauline theology often externalizes divinity, portraying God as distant and humanity as unworthy. Paul's lament in **Romans 7:18** illustrates this dichotomy when he says, "*For I know that **good itself does not dwell in me**, that is, in my sinful nature.*" This perspective obscures the inner divinity that Jesus consistently highlighted, fostering a worldview of disconnection rather than unity.

The Law of One teaches that each soul is eternal and inherently connected to the One Source, with physical life serving as a temporary experience within the greater whole. Jesus' words in **John 8:58** reflect this timeless unity when he says, *"Before Abraham was, I AM."* By invoking the eternal "*I AM*," Jesus identifies with the infinite and timeless nature of the Divine. In contrast, Paul's writings often focus on a future-oriented salvation, as seen in **1 Corinthians 15:42-44**, where he describes the resurrection of the body as a transformative event yet to come. This forward-looking emphasis detracts from the eternal now and the ever-present unity with the Source that Jesus affirmed.

The Law of One invites us to live in alignment with these principles, transforming our understanding of self, others, and the Divine. To embrace this perspective we must first recognize Oneness by challenging dualistic thinking, and see all beings as interconnected expressions of the One Infinite Creator. Then we must live life with Love and Service to Others by prioritizing acts of compassion and selflessness. In this way we recognize that serving others is serving the Divine. Finally, we must seek our own divine inner connection by cultivating practices such as meditation and prayer to awaken the presence of God within.

Jesus' teachings reveal a vision of unity, love, and divine immanence that transcends the limitations of Pauline theology. The Law of One provides a lens through which we can rediscover the essence of Christ's message, liberating ourselves from fear-based doctrines and embracing the transformative power of divine oneness. By understanding and living these truths, we align with the eternal reality that Jesus came to reveal: that all is One.

The Law of One Prayer of Christ

One of the most overlooked yet profoundly powerful moments in the entire New Testament is found in the Gospel of John, chapter 17. Here, just before his arrest, Jesus lifts his eyes to heaven and offers what is often referred to as his "high priestly prayer." But when read through the lens of Christ Consciousness and the Law of One, this prayer becomes something far more: it is a declaration of divine unity.

John 17:21 – "That they may all be one; even as You, Father, are in Me and I in You, that they also may be in Us…"

This statement is the very essence of the Law of One: that all is One, and that separation is an illusion born of ego and fear. In this prayer, Christ affirms that just as He is one with the Father, so too can we become one with the Divine. He makes no distinction between himself and the awakened potential in all of us. His words are not those of exclusivity, but of profound inclusivity.

This is not a call to worship Jesus as a distant deity, but an invitation to awaken the same Divine presence within ourselves. It is a reminder that **the Kingdom of God is within us**, and that by aligning with divine love, we become conduits of that same oneness.

In this single chapter, we see the clearest articulation of Christ Consciousness in the entire Bible: a direct, heartfelt plea that humanity remember its divine origin and return to unity with Source. Jesus was not simply praying for his disciples. He was praying for all of us.

John 17:20 – "I do not ask for these only, but also for those who will believe in me through their word."

This is the Christ speaking not from separation, but from union. From Oneness. From Love. And in doing so, he gives voice to the deepest prayer of the soul: to return to the Source from which it came, and to realize that it never truly left.

Chapter-7: Reincarnation

Many within the Christian church contend that reincarnation is incompatible with Jesus' teachings, often labeling it a "lie from the devil." They will typically point to the following verse as their main argument against the concept of reincarnation:

Hebrews 9:27 – *"And as it is appointed unto men once to die, but after this the judgment"*

At first glance, this verse appears to refute reincarnation by stating that men die only once. However, as with many scriptures, examining a single verse in isolation risks overlooking the broader context in which it was written. Here is a little more of the context for the reader to consider:

Hebrews 9:25-28 – *"Nor yet that he [Jesus] should offer himself often, as the high priest entereth into the holy place every year with blood of others; For then must he often have suffered since the foundation of the world: but now once in the end of the world hath he appeared to put away sin by the sacrifice of himself. And as it is appointed unto men once to die, but after this the judgment: So Christ was once offered to bear the sins of many; and unto them that look for him shall he appear the second time without sin unto salvation."*

So, the author was drawing a comparison to the differences between the Old Covenant, and the New Covenant. In the Old Covenant, people would have to sacrifice a lamb once a year to cover or atone for their sins. During the ceremony the high priest would have to enter the "Holy of Holies", which was the place where the Ark of the Covenant was housed, to sprinkle blood on the altar to cover the sins of the people. However, according to the new covenant, Jesus' blood was shed once and for all, with no need to continue with the old covenant sacrifices. So, the picture which the author was trying to paint was that Jesus only had to do this once instead of over and over again every year, not necessarily that reincarnation is false. However, this verse remains to be the most common refutation of reincarnation used to this day by the Church.

Also to consider is the fact that this scripture actually doesn't conflict with a common notion of reincarnation. The phrase "*it is appointed unto men once to die, but after this the judgment*" aligns closely with the concept of a life-review process, often described by those who have experienced near-death phenomena. Thus, this process would be expected to happen for each life lived through reincarnation. With regards to that individual incarnation, it would be true that a man would die once, and then be given a life-review, which the author calls "judgment". Then at some point that spirit would reincarnate into another life, and the process would be repeated.

Few realize that Jesus himself referenced what can be interpreted as nothing less than an example of reincarnation in the Bible. First, let us read the scripture from the book of Luke where the "Angel of the Lord" was speaking to the high priest Zacharias about the coming of his son who would ultimately grow up to become John the Baptist.

Luke 1:13-17 – "*But the angel said unto him, Fear not, Zacharias: for thy prayer is heard; and thy wife Elisabeth shall bear thee a son, and thou shalt call his name John. And thou shalt have joy and gladness; and many shall rejoice at his birth. For he shall be great in the sight of the Lord, and shall drink neither wine nor strong drink; and **he shall be filled with the Holy Ghost**, even from his mother's womb. And many of the children of Israel shall he turn to the Lord their God. And he shall go before him in the **spirit and power of Elijah**, to turn the hearts of the fathers to the children, and the disobedient to the wisdom of the just; to make ready a people prepared for the Lord.*"

The Angel of the Lord's statement, "*And he shall go before him in the* **spirit and power of Elijah**," can be interpreted as suggesting that John embodied the essence or spirit of Elijah in a new incarnation. However, this is not the standard Christian doctrinal stance, so let us look to see if there is any other corroboration of this idea in the scriptures.

In the book of Matthew, there are several references to John the Baptist that challenge the conventional belief that reincarnation is "a lie from the devil." The first passage is from the book of Matthew:

Matthew 11:7-15 - "*As they departed, Jesus began to say to the multitudes concerning John: 'What did you go out into the wilderness to see? A reed shaken by the wind? But what did you go out to see? A man clothed in soft garments? Indeed, those who wear soft clothing are in kings' houses. But what did you go out to see? A prophet? Yes, I say to you, and **more than a prophet**. For this is he of whom it is written: 'Behold, I send My messenger before Your face, who will prepare Your way before You.' Assuredly, I say to you, **among those born of women there has not risen one greater than John the Baptist**; but he who is least in the kingdom of heaven is greater than he. And from the days of John the Baptist until now the kingdom of heaven suffers violence, and the violent take it by force. For all the prophets and the law prophesied until John. And if you are willing to receive it, **he is Elijah** who is to come. **He who has ears to hear, let him hear!**"*

In verse 15, Jesus plainly said that John the Baptist was Elijah the prophet. He even used the statement, "*He who has ears to hear, let him hear!*", which is a phrase that, when used by Jesus, indicates a profound spiritual truth, one that only those attuned to the Spirit would understand. This is a clear indication that John was the reincarnation or return of Elijah.

So, why did John himself refute being Elijah when asked directly? In **John 1:21**, John the Baptist denies being Elijah, but this denial likely stems from his desire not to draw attention to himself or his mission. John's purpose was to prepare the way for Christ, not to elevate his own identity. He understood that while he fulfilled the prophetic role of Elijah, he was not the "person" of Elijah in this particular incarnation. In essence, he was John, fulfilling the role of Elijah through divine appointment, but humbly redirecting attention from himself to the

Messiah. This understanding becomes even clearer when we turn to the book of Malachi:

Malachi 3:1 – "*Behold, **I will send my messenger, who will prepare the way before me**. Then suddenly the Lord you are seeking will come to his temple; the messenger of the covenant, whom you desire, will come,' says the Lord Almighty.*"

Malachi 4:5-6 – "*Behold, **I will send you Elijah the prophet** before the coming of the great and dreadful day of the LORD: And he shall turn the heart of the fathers to the children, and the heart of the children to their fathers, lest I come and smite the earth with a curse.*"

Here, Malachi clearly foretells that Elijah would return before the coming of the Lord, preparing the way for the Messiah. Jesus' words in Matthew verify this prophecy and further clarify John's identity as Elijah:

Matthew 17:10-13 – "*And His disciples asked Him, saying, 'Why then do the scribes say that Elijah must come first?' Jesus answered and said to them, 'Indeed, Elijah is coming first and will restore all things. But I say to you that **Elijah has come already**, and they did not know him but did to him whatever they wished. Likewise the Son of Man is also about to suffer at their hands.' **Then the disciples understood that He spoke to them of John the Baptist.**"*

With this final affirmation from Jesus himself, we see that John the Baptist was indeed the return of Elijah. However, John's own humble denial of being Elijah in his physical form does not negate this reality; instead, it reflects John's deep commitment to his mission of pointing the way to Christ.

When we apply the concept of reincarnation to the other principles of Christianity, it actually becomes a missing piece of the puzzle in many ways. Yet, there is one place where the concept of reincarnation makes the biggest difference in my mind. It answers the one remaining conflict in Christianity that I had wrestled with for years, which we have discussed previously. You may remember the question from an earlier chapter on the Omnipotence of God:

"On one side there's the belief that God is truly omnipotent, all-knowing, all-powerful, and all-good. However, how could an omnipotent God create a race of beings who for the most part, based on the "doctrine" of Christianity, would live out their lives on Earth in a painful existence, and the majority of them would be doomed to eternal torment in a place called Hell. That just does not equate to a good God in my mind."

Applying the concept of reincarnation to this question resolves many of these apparent conflicts, offering a more coherent understanding of divine justice and human experience. Rather than limiting individuals to a single lifetime to align with divine will, reincarnation provides the opportunity for spiritual growth across multiple lifetimes, aligning more closely with the concept of an omnipotent and benevolent God. Understanding reincarnation as part of a divine plan fundamentally reshapes how we view life, death, and spiritual growth.

The application of the concept of Reincarnation potentially answers the question of why the Hindu deity of Krishna had lived a life so similar to Jesus Christ? Perhaps Jesus was just another incarnation of the exact same "Spirit" of the messianic entity who had been Krishna? This would certainly explain why their stories were almost identical.

The Many Lives of Christ

Maurice Cotterell, a British engineer, scientist, and author, is renowned for his innovative theories that intertwine science, spirituality, and ancient history. One of his most intriguing theories is presented in his book *The Many Lives of Jesus*, where he posits that Christ was not a singular historical figure but rather a recurring divine being who manifested in different cultures and times throughout history[68].

---

[68] Maurice Cotterell, *The Many Lives of Jesus: The Christ Revealed* (London: Piatkus, 2004), 5–10.

Cotterell's theory suggests that Christ has reincarnated across various epochs, each time imparting a message of love and compassion tailored to humanity's needs. Cotterell's initial breakthrough which started him on this path was the decoding of the treasures found in the tomb of the great Mayan king Lord Pacal in the Temple of the Inscriptions at the ancient Maya site of Palenque, situated in the state of Chiapas, Mexico. He determined that Lord Pacal knew about what Cotterell calls the "Super Science of the Sun" based on the fact that the information was encoded in many of the treasures, including the lid of his sarcophagus which Cotterell calls the "Amazing Lid of Palenque"[69].

Central to Cotterell's theory is the belief that Christ represents a divine being who has reincarnated throughout history, manifesting in diverse cultures and epochs to guide humanity's spiritual evolution. He proposes that the same soul that incarnated as Jesus also manifested in other significant spiritual leaders throughout history. According to Cotterell, these reincarnations were part of a divine plan to guide humanity through different phases of spiritual and moral development. Each incarnation served to impart teachings of love, compassion, and wisdom, tailored to the needs of the people at that particular time.

Cotterell identifies several historical figures who he believes are incarnations of the same divine soul that later became known as Jesus. These figures include:

- Lord Krishna: The Hindu god and teacher
- Tutankhamun: The young pharaoh of Egypt.
- Buddha: The founder of Buddhism
- Quetzalcoatl: The feathered serpent god of the Mesoamerica
- Lord Pacal: The Mayan king whose tomb is at Palenque.
- Viracocha: The creator god of the Inca civilization.
- Jesus: The central figure of Christianity.

---

[69] Maurice Cotterell, *The Many Lives of Jesus: The Christ Revealed* (London: Piatkus, 2004), 15–20.

Cotterell is known for his work on sunspot cycles and their influence on humanity. He discovered that sunspots follow a cyclical pattern, and that these cycles influence the rise and fall of civilizations, as well as the timing of divine incarnations. In "The Many Lives of Jesus", he suggests that the timing of these reincarnations is linked to solar activity, and the corresponding effects on the Earth's electromagnetic field. Cotterell's theory posits that ancient civilizations, particularly the Maya, had a deep understanding of these solar cycles. He argues that their knowledge was encoded in their calendar, architecture, and artifacts, such as the Lid of Palenque[70]. Cotterell believes the lid contains messages about these recurring incarnations of the divine being. He states that the Mayan Calendar was based on these solar sunspot cycles.

One of Cotterell's most famous interpretations is of the sarcophagus lid of Lord Pacal. Cotterell suggests that the intricate carvings on the lid contain encoded information about the cycles of sunspots and the reincarnations of the divine soul. He interprets the imagery as depicting not only Lord Pacal's life but also a broader cosmological story that includes the many lives of Jesus. Cotterell argues that the lid of Pacal's tomb reveals that Lord Pacal was one of the incarnations of the same divine soul that was Jesus. He believes that the Mayans were aware of this connection, and they encoded it into their art and architecture.

Cotterell's theory is closely related to the concept of Christ Consciousness, which suggests that the person of Jesus was not unique in his divine nature, but rather an exemplar of a universal spiritual state that had incarnated as others. Cotterell argues that the soul that incarnated as Jesus was an embodiment of this Christ Consciousness, and that it manifested in different forms throughout history to guide humanity. According to Cotterell, the purpose of these incarnations was to assist in the spiritual evolution of humanity, helping people to transcend material concerns and attain a higher state of

---

[70] Maurice Cotterell, *The Many Lives of Jesus: The Christ Revealed* (London: Piatkus, 2004), 45–50.

consciousness. He suggests that by studying the lives of these incarnations, we can gain insights into our own spiritual path.

One of the central points in Cotterell's theory is that all these incarnations, including Jesus, taught a universal message of love, compassion, and the importance of living a righteous life. He suggests that by recognizing the commonality in these teachings across different cultures, humanity can move toward a more unified and enlightened existence. Cotterell believes that the recurring incarnation of this divine being is part of a larger divine plan, to guide humanity through various stages of development. Each incarnation is seen as a response to the specific needs and challenges of the time, helping to steer humanity toward greater spiritual awareness.

Cotterell's theories on the many lives of Christ align with the belief that Christ's soul has incarnated throughout history to guide humanity. This perspective sets the stage for understanding Christ's role not just in biblical times but in the deeper history of human consciousness.

The Law of One: Cayce's Insights

Edgar Cayce, often referred to as the "Sleeping Prophet," was one of the most renowned psychics of the 20th century. His trance readings covered a wide range of topics, including health, spirituality, and ancient civilizations. Among his most fascinating contributions are his insights into Atlantis, reincarnation, and humanity's spiritual evolution. Cayce's readings on the Law of One describe it as a spiritual philosophy emphasizing unity, divine love, and the interconnectedness of all creation. These readings offer a profound look at the forces shaping human history and consciousness.

Building on this idea, the Law of One represents a universal truth that spans cultures and eras, emphasizing unity, love, and the interconnectedness of all existence. While the 1981 Ra Material introduced many readers to this concept, Edgar Cayce's earlier readings also spoke of the Law of One in the context of Atlantis, linking it to profound spiritual teachings and practices. Cayce's insights reveal

Christ as a central figure in the Law of One, working alongside others to guide humanity through a period of immense transformation.

According to Cayce, the Children of the Law of One were a spiritually advanced group in Atlantis, dedicated to preserving divine unity and harmony and service to others. This group opposed the Sons of Belial[71], who prioritized materialism, self-interest, and the misuse of advanced technologies for personal gain in service to self. According to Cayce Christ, in one of his many incarnations, served as a spiritual leader for the Children of the Law of One. His mission was to embody and teach the principles of divine oneness, guiding humanity back to alignment with Universal Consciousness.

Cayce's readings describe the Atlantean struggle as a microcosm of a broader cosmic battle between light and shadow. The teachings of the Law of One, championed by Christ and the Children of the Law of One, sought to counteract the destructive tendencies of the Sons of Belial and redirect humanity toward spiritual ascension.

The Great Pyramid as a Tool for Ascension

Both Cayce's readings and the Ra Material attribute profound significance to the Great Pyramid, describing it as more than a mere architectural wonder. Cayce claimed that the Great Pyramid was constructed under the guidance of Ra Ta, Hermes, and other enlightened beings from Atlantis. These architects imbued the Pyramid with sacred geometry and energetic properties designed to facilitate spiritual initiation and healing.

The Ra Material echoes this narrative, describing the Pyramid as a "crystallized" structure that harnessed cosmic energies to aid in the spiritual evolution of individuals. It functioned as a focal point for healing, meditation, and connecting with higher realms of consciousness. Together, Cayce's and Ra's accounts underscore the Pyramid's role as a bridge between the physical and spiritual

---

[71] Edgar Cayce, *Edgar Cayce on Atlantis*, edited by Hugh Lynn Cayce (New York: A.R.E. Press, 1968), 45–49.

dimensions, a tool created by those aligned with the Law of One to uplift humanity.

Thoth and the Wisdom of the Law of One

The figure of Thoth occupies a central role in the transmission of Atlantean wisdom to later civilizations. Edgar Cayce's readings suggest that Thoth was an Atlantean priest-king who carried forward the teachings of the Law of One after the destruction of Atlantis. As a master of sacred geometry, alchemy, and mystical knowledge, Thoth laid the spiritual and intellectual foundation for the great civilization of Egypt.

Thoth's wisdom was instrumental in shaping the spiritual practices and architectural achievements of ancient Egypt. According to Cayce, Thoth played a key role in constructing temples and other structures designed to preserve the knowledge of Atlantis and align humanity with divine principles. His teachings were encoded in texts such as the *Emerald Tablets*, which emphasize the interconnectedness of all life and the path to spiritual enlightenment.

Cayce's description of Thoth's mission aligns with the principles of Christ Consciousness, which are service to others, spiritual unity, and the pursuit of higher understanding. By guiding humanity through periods of darkness and rediscovering the divine spark within, Thoth's work echoes the broader mission of Christ Consciousness. His role as a preserver of the Law of One underscores his alignment with these universal truths.

Hermes Trismegistus and the Great Pyramid

The connection between Thoth and Hermes Trismegistus bridges ancient Egyptian wisdom and the Hermetic tradition that emerged centuries later. Cayce identified Hermes as a pivotal figure in the construction of the Great Pyramid[72], working alongside Ra Ta and

---

[72] Edgar Cayce, *Edgar Cayce's Egypt: Psychic Revelations on the Most Fascinating Civilization Ever Known*, edited by Edgar Evans Cayce (New York: A.R.E. Press, 2004), 112–15.

others to create a structure that would endure as a tool for spiritual initiation.

Cayce's readings describe the Great Pyramid as a physical manifestation of Hermetic principles, reflecting the cosmic order through its precise alignment and sacred geometry. Hermes and his collaborators designed the Pyramid to serve as a center for spiritual initiation, healing, and enlightenment.[73] Its chambers and passageways symbolically represent the soul's journey toward unity with the Creator.

The Ra Material reinforces this perspective, describing the Pyramid as a "crystallized thought-form" that amplifies spiritual energy. Both sources emphasize the Pyramid's role in fostering the evolution of consciousness, providing a space for individuals to connect with higher dimensions and integrate the teachings of the Law of One. Through his role as the architect of the Great Pyramid, Hermes Trismegistus preserved the wisdom of Atlantis and the Law of One, ensuring that these truths would endure through the ages.

---

[73] John Van Auken and Lora Little, *Edgar Cayce's Tales of Ancient Egypt* (Virginia Beach: A.R.E. Press, 2000), 94–98.

Chapter-8: Christ Consciousness: The Christ in You

This chapter invites readers to deepen their understanding of Christ, presenting not a departure from faith but its profound expansion. Many know Jesus as a teacher and savior, who embodied divine love and wisdom, yet His life and words often hint at an even greater mystery: a call for each of us to realize our own divine potential. Christ's message, as seen through a broader lens, encourages us to awaken to our inherent connection to God and to embody the qualities He demonstrated such as compassion, wisdom, and love.

To grasp Jesus' self-understanding, we must transcend the labels and doctrines imposed over centuries. The idea of Christ Consciousness does not diminish the reverence for Jesus; instead, it brings us closer to the essence of His teachings by recognizing the divine spark within all people. As Christ Himself expressed, "*I am in the Father, and the Father is in me*". This is a profound truth that points toward our own potential for unity with the Divine.

Jesus' teaching, "***Judge not****, lest you be judged*," reflects a message centered on inclusion, compassion, and transformative love. This chapter encourages you, particularly those who have dedicated their lives to following His example, to consider that true faith is a living, growing experience. By aligning with Christ's essence, His Christ Consciousness, we open ourselves to the possibility of profound spiritual growth, rooted in love and free from fear.

I urge readers, especially pastors and spiritual leaders, to explore these truths personally, inviting the Spirit to unveil what resonates deeply within their hearts. After all, Faith is a journey of discovery. My hope is to inspire reflection, not doubt; unity, not division. Through the light of Christ's message, we can move beyond fear and embrace love, recognizing the divinity that resides within each of us.

The concept of Christ Consciousness is a state of spiritual awareness and understanding that embodies Love, Compassion, and True

Enlightenment, in a state of complete union with the Divine. It is most often associated with the life and teachings of Yeshua "The Christ", who came to show us "The Way" of being which is Christ Consciousness. For that is what he truly meant when he said, "*I am in the Father, and the Father is in me.*"

However, he did not simply come to BE our "Savior", but to show us how we can also become one with the Divine. By following the example He set before us, we all can achieve a level of Christ Consciousness within ourselves. For as Yeshua said, "*Truly, truly, I say to you, whoever believes in me* **will also do the works that I do; and greater works than these will he do**..."

Among the most well-known biblical verses, **John 3:16** declares, "*For God so loved the world that He gave His only begotten Son, that whoever believes in Him should not perish but have everlasting life.*" Rendered in Aramaic, the language spoken by Jesus, **John 3:16** unveils a profound and richly nuanced expression of divine love. This verse takes on an even deeper resonance when we look at the meaning behind the Aramaic words.

"*For the Divine Love so deeply cherished and protected the world, that He sent His beloved and unique Son, so that everyone who intimately trusts in Him would not find themselves lost, but would* **awaken to unending life and unity with the Divine**."

This rendering shows us a vision of God's love as an active, sustaining force that holds creation together with compassion and intention. The Aramaic word for "love" used here is "khaziq".[74] It suggests not only affection but an abiding, protective love. A love that is actively engaged in the world, nurturing and guiding it. Further, the phrase "*believes in Him*" carries an implication beyond intellectual belief. In Aramaic, it translates more closely to "embrace with faith," pointing to faith as a living relationship. Trust in Christ becomes a path to unity with the

---

[74] Neil Douglas-Klotz, *Prayers of the Cosmos: Meditations on the Aramaic Words of Jesus* (San Francisco: HarperOne, 1990), 45-48.

Divine, an intimate connection rather than simply a matter of belief. Lastly, the term haiyaya (eternal life) isn't just about life after death; it speaks to a fuller, richer life that begins here and now. It suggests a life in divine purpose and consciousness in a state unification with God's own life, something that transcends time and endures eternally.

In this context, **John 3:16** becomes not just a promise of salvation, but an invitation to awaken to a higher way of living. By trusting in the Divine and embracing the teachings of Christ, we are drawn into a life filled with love, purpose, and an enduring connection to God. Through this lens, eternal life is not only endless but deeply meaningful, a shared life with the Divine that reflects God's own love for the world.

From Sin Consciousness to Christ Consciousness

Humanity's spiritual journey hinges on a fundamental choice between two diametrically opposing forces: **Fear** and **Love**. These forces underpin two theological paradigms that have profoundly shaped Christianity, which are the **fear-based doctrine of sin consciousness** and the **Love-based Truth of Christ Consciousness**. Understanding the origins and impacts of these paradigms is essential to uncovering the transformative power of Jesus' teachings and freeing billions trapped in the dogmatic frameworks of Pauline theology and the Roman Catholic Church.

The concept of sin consciousness stems from the belief that humanity is intrinsically flawed and perpetually separated from God. Rooted in Pauline theology, this paradigm uses **fear** as its primary motivator. Fear manifests in various ways, beginning with the fear of judgment. Pauline theology emphasizes humanity's guilt before God, as seen in **Romans 3:23**, which states, "*For all have sinned and fall short of the glory of God.*" This fosters anxiety about divine wrath and eternal punishment, creating a transactional relationship with God where salvation is sought through external acts of confession and belief.

This fear of judgment is closely tied to the fear of separation, perpetuated by the doctrine of original sin. It enforces the narrative that humanity is born in a state of separation from God, inherently flawed and incapable of divine connection without external mediation. Such a worldview perpetuates guilt and shame, trapping individuals in a cycle of dependency on religious institutions for absolution. **Fear** also serves as a **powerful control mechanism** wielded by hierarchical systems and forces of negative polarity. By keeping individuals focused on their inadequacies and the threat of punishment, sin consciousness suppresses spiritual growth and blinds individuals to their innate connection to the divine.

In stark contrast, **Christ Consciousness** offers a liberating path grounded in the **love**-centered teachings of Jesus. Love, not fear, becomes the primary mover and the essence of divine truth. Jesus consistently taught that God is not distant but intimately present within each individual. In **John 14:20**, Jesus declared, "*I am in the Father, and you are in me, and I am in you*," affirming divine unity and interconnectedness. Similarly, in **Luke 17:21**, he proclaimed, "*The kingdom of God is within you*," underscoring that humanity is not inherently separated from God but deeply connected to the divine, capable of embodying God's love and purpose.

Jesus' message of **love** emphasizes transformation rather than fear-driven compliance. His call to repentance is not about guilt but a joyous realignment with divine purpose. Through acts of service, compassion, and forgiveness, individuals express divine love and live in harmony with God's will. This is encapsulated in Jesus' teaching on the greatest commandments, as seen in **Matthew 22:37-39**: "*Love the Lord your God with all your heart, with all your soul, and with all your mind. This is the first and greatest commandment. And the second is like it: Love your neighbor as yourself.*" The key to this scripture is the fact that the Divine resides in **YOU**! Thus, in order for you to love the divine with everything that you are, you must first be able to **Love Yourself**. Then you will realize that the divine spark is truly within all of us, which will allow you to love your neighbor as yourself.

Love also empowers individuals to see themselves as co-creators with God, capable of embodying divine attributes like kindness, humility, and forgiveness. Again, this comes by way of realizing the divine within yourself, allowing you to truly believe that you are a creator, because you are part of the Creator. By embracing this truth, individuals transcend fear and live authentically, free from external control and aligned with divine will. Christ Consciousness reveals that God's presence within each person is a source of infinite strength and creativity, inspiring transformation and the realization of one's highest potential.

The contrast between Pauline theology and the teachings of Jesus further highlights the divergence between sin consciousness and Christ Consciousness. Pauline theology, rooted in fear, frames humanity as inherently sinful and in need of external salvation through Jesus' sacrificial death. It emphasizes confession and belief as the path to salvation while de-emphasizing moral transformation of self and acts of unconditional love towards others. This doctrine presents God as wrathful, requiring payment for sin to satisfy divine justice. In stark contrast, Jesus' teachings proclaim **divine unity** and the presence of **God within each individual**. They present God as a loving and forgiving parent who seeks reconciliation rather than retribution. Remember the parable of the Prodigal Son! Jesus calls for repentance, obedience, and service as expressions of love and pathways to spiritual fulfillment. These all become natural free expressions once you put off the chains of sin consciousness and embrace the freedom of Christ Consciousness.

The core contrast between fear and love reveals their vastly different impacts on the human spirit. Fear thrives on the illusion of separation, convincing individuals that they are unworthy and dependent on external structures for salvation. It reinforces hierarchical systems that exploit guilt and shame to maintain power. In sin consciousness, fear keeps individuals trapped in spiritual stagnation, blind to their divine potential. Love, on the other hand, dissolves the illusion of separation and affirms that God's presence is within each person, emanating a spirit of oneness. It empowers individuals to take responsibility for their spiritual journey, living authentically and in harmony with others. In Christ Consciousness, love liberates by revealing the truth of divine unity and the infinite potential within each soul.

To break free from sin consciousness and embrace Christ Consciousness, individuals must recognize the illusion of separation and the ever-present unity with the **One** as **God**. By rejecting fear-based doctrines and choosing love as their guiding principle, we can move beyond the control mechanisms that perpetuate guilt and dependency. Jesus' teachings provide a clear pathway by focusing on the **Gospel of Love** through repentance, obedience, and service, and living out his command to love God and neighbor. Practices such as meditation and mindful reflection on the divine presence nurture awareness and strengthen the connection to God.

The choice between sin consciousness and Christ Consciousness is a choice between **fear** and **love**, control and freedom, separation and unity. Jesus' message was not one of guilt and punishment but of empowerment and divine union. By embracing Christ Consciousness, individuals can break free from the cycle of fear and live in alignment with the liberating truth of God's love. As Jesus proclaimed in **John 8:32**, "*You will know the **truth**, and the **truth** will set you **free**.*" This truth inspires a return to the Gospel of Love, where fear gives way to freedom, and love reigns supreme.

The Hermetic Synthesis

The Hermetic teachings encapsulated in the phrase "As above, so below" resonate deeply with the concept of Christ Consciousness. Both traditions underscore self-knowledge, the recognition of one's divine essence, and the transcendence of ignorance. The Hermetic path is one of awakening, where we learn to see beyond the illusions of the material world, and recognize our unity with the Divine.[75]

Integrating these insights fosters the alchemical transformation described in Hermeticism, turning the lead of human limitation into the gold of divine consciousness. This is the path to becoming, not just followers of a spiritual tradition, but true embodiments of the Christ

---

[75] Elaine Pagels, *The Gnostic Gospels* (New York: Random House, 1979), 84-89.

Consciousness, living examples of the divine truth that we are all one with the Infinite Mind.

Hermeticism is derived from the teachings attributed to **Hermes Trismegistus**, a figure believed to be a synthesis of the Greek god **Hermes** and his earlier incarnation as the Egyptian god **Thoth**, both associated with wisdom, writing, and knowledge. Hermeticism combines elements of Neoplatonism, Gnosticism, and ancient Egyptian spirituality, focusing on themes like the divine unity of all existence, the pursuit of gnosis, and the correspondence between the macrocosm (universe) and microcosm (individual).

In the Gospel of Mary, Jesus declares, "***There is no sin***," challenging traditional perceptions of sin as an inherent moral failing. Instead, it aligns with the Hermetic principle that all perceived flaws or "sins" are rooted in ignorance of our divine nature, and the true nature of reality. In the Hermetics Principle of Mentalism, sin is not a transgression against a divine law, but a misunderstanding or misalignment with the divine truth that we are all fractal aspects of the One Mind, the source of all creation.[76]

The Gospel of Philip reinforces this by stating, "*Ignorance is the mother of all evil.*" This echoes the Hermetic understanding that evil is not a force unto itself, but a **lack of knowledge**, a shadow cast by the absence of light. In Hermetics, the process of spiritual awakening involves dispelling ignorance and aligning our consciousness with the higher truths of the universe. This awakening allows us to transcend the illusion of separation, and recognize our unity with the divine.[77]

The concept of reincarnation, embraced by many early Christians, also has deep Hermetic roots. As we discussed earlier, Jesus proclaimed reincarnation when he said John the Baptist was Elijah reborn. This belief is harmonious with the Hermetic understanding of the soul's

---

[76] Karen L. King, *The Gospel of Mary of Magdala: Jesus and the First Woman Apostle* (Santa Rosa, CA: Polebridge Press, 2003), 23-26.
[77] Willis Barnstone and Marvin Meyer, *The Gnostic Bible* (Boston: Shambhala, 2003), 155-160.

journey through multiple lifetimes. According to Hermetics, the soul evolves through cycles of birth, death, and rebirth, continually refining itself until it achieves mastery and unity with the Divine.

Hermetics teaches that the material world is a realm of learning and transformation. Through the Principle of Correspondence, we understand that our experiences in the physical world are reflections of higher spiritual realities. Reincarnation is a process by which the soul, through successive lives, gains the knowledge and wisdom necessary to return to its divine source, transcending the cycle of rebirth once it fully realizes its divine nature.[78]

Christ Consciousness and the True Identity of Jesus

Perhaps the most profound teaching suppressed by the Roman Catholic Church is the true nature of Jesus, as conveyed in the Gnostic texts. Rather than an exclusive Son of God, Jesus is depicted as a divine exemplar, demonstrating the potential inherent in all humanity to awaken to their divine nature. This teaching aligns with the Hermetic principle of Divine Oneness, which asserts that all beings emanate from the One Mind, sharing the potential to realize their divine essence.

In the Gospel of Thomas, Jesus declares, "**We are all** *Sons of the living Father*," inviting recognition of the divine presence within every individual. Hermetics emphasizes that the divine spark exists in all things, and that our spiritual journey is about awakening to this truth. The Christ Consciousness that Jesus embodied is not an external or unique quality, but an inner state of being that we all can ultimately achieve. For as Jesus himself told us, "*Verily, verily, I say unto you, He that believeth on me,* **the works that I do shall he do also; and greater works than these shall he do;**"

The Gospel of Philip's declaration that "*this person is* **no longer a Christian but a Christ**" speaks to the transformative power of this

---

[78] Elaine Pagels, *The Gnostic Gospels* (New York: Random House, 1979), 65-70.

realization. In Hermetics, this transformation is the goal of the spiritual path, thus transcending the limitations of the ego, the material world, and even religious identity, to embody the divine essence fully. This is the ultimate alchemical process, the transmutation of the soul from base ignorance to divine wisdom, from mere human to Christ-like consciousness.[79]

Again, in the Gospel of Thomas, Christ says, "*Whoever drinks from my mouth **will become like me; I myself shall become that person**, and the hidden things will be revealed to him.*" This profound statement encapsulates the essence of Christ Consciousness, which is the transformative journey of awakening to one's inherent divinity. To "**drink from my mouth**" is to internalize the wisdom, truth, and divine essence that Jesus embodied. It signifies a direct, unmediated relationship with the divine, and a mystical communion that transcends dogma and ritual.

When Jesus declares, "*I myself shall become that person*," he reveals a central mystery of the spiritual path, which is the dissolution of the separation between the individual and the divine. This is not simply a metaphor but a call to recognize the unity that underlies all existence. In becoming "*like me*," the disciple does not merely imitate Jesus but embodies the Christ Consciousness, realizing their oneness with the Universal Mind.

Furthermore, the assurance that "*the **hidden** things will be **revealed**"* emphasizes the uncovering of profound spiritual truths, often concealed by materialism, ego, and traditional dogma. This revelation is the awakening to the divine spark within, the realization that the ultimate truth of existence is found not in external doctrines but in the transformative light of inner gnosis.

This insight resonates with the Hermetic principle of "As above, so below," reflecting the universal truth that the divine nature of Christ resides within every individual. It also echoes the alchemical journey of

---

[79] Willis Barnstone and Marvin Meyer, *The Gnostic Bible* (Boston: Shambhala, 2003), 170-175.

turning lead into gold, which is a metaphor for transcending the mundane and realizing the sacred. To fully embody this Christ-like state is to bridge the gap between the human and the divine, achieving what the Gospel of Philip so powerfully describes as becoming "*no longer a Christian but **a Christ**.*"

This understanding not only illuminates the true identity of Jesus but also empowers every seeker to transcend their perceived limitations. It is a call to action, a reminder that the teachings of Jesus are not about worshiping a figure but about becoming one with the divine essence he manifested. In this, the true revolutionary power of Christ Consciousness is revealed. A power that invites us to step into our highest potential and to transform both ourselves and the world around us.

As we begin to reclaim the true identity of Christ, not as a distant savior but as the embodiment of divine consciousness within, it becomes equally important to recognize how these deeper truths have been preserved in unexpected places. Sometimes, they were hidden in plain sight, encoded not in scripture, but in art. One such example is Leonardo da Vinci's Last Supper, which may contain one of the most profound visual representations of the true spiritual message of Christ.

The Sacred Message in Da Vinci's Last Supper

Another insight worth considering is Leonardo da Vinci's masterful painting The Last Supper, which may encode a deeper esoteric message, one aligned with the true teaching of Christ Consciousness. If we look carefully, we see the figure to Jesus' right (traditionally said to be the apostle John) is clearly feminine. She wears garments of pink and blue, which are symbolic colors of the sacred feminine and masculine in balance. Her hands are gently folded in a posture that closely resembles the mudra of Intuition. In contrast, Peter, who leans toward her, wears a sour expression on his face and holds a knife behind Judas' back while gesturing toward her throat with his left hand, implying suppression of the feminine voice.

Even more striking are the mirrored hand gestures made by Jesus and Judas on either side of the feminine figure. Jesus' right hand and Judas' left are extended in matching inverted poses, palms down in the pose of the mudra of creation. In this Da Vinci may have been symbolizing the idea that all of this physical creation is founded on the concept of polarity, with Jesus reflecting the Positive polarity of Service-to-others and Judas representing the negative polarity of Service-to-self, embodied by the fact that he holds a bag of silver in his right hand. Between them, Mary's hands rest in a centered, prayer-like gesture of stillness and gnosis. This triad of Jesus, Mary, and Judas forms a powerful visual metaphor: creation, betrayal, and balance. It reveals that duality (as seen in Judas and Jesus) can only be harmonized through the wisdom of the Divine Feminine through gnosis.

Da Vinci, a student of sacred geometry and hidden meaning, seems to be showing us that Mary Magdalene, long maligned or erased, may have been the 13th and most important disciple: the one who truly understood Christ. Some researchers have even proposed that Da Vinci intentionally left out the apostle John altogether, replacing him with Mary to make a symbolic point. If true, this omission would be especially poignant when considering that the Gospel of John was written much later than the other three synoptic gospels and reflects a theology far more aligned with the doctrines of Paul than with the original teachings of Jesus. Many biblical scholars have questioned the authorship of the Gospel of John for this reason, suggesting it may have been composed in part to validate and reinforce Pauline theology, which was beginning to dominate the early Christian narrative.

This interpretation not only restores the feminine to her rightful place but also echoes the teaching that balance is the key to transcendence. Christ Consciousness arises not by rejecting polarity, but by integrating it through Love.

Let us continue exploring other revelations that bring us closer to the Truth hidden in plain sight.

The Holy Trinity

The concept of the Trinity often brings to mind Christ's words in "The Great Commission" (**Matthew 28:19**), where He instructed His disciples to baptize "*in the name of the **Father**, and of the **Son**, and of the **Holy Spirit**,*" emphasizing the equality and unity of the three persons.

In Paul's letters he often refers to the three persons in close association, such as in **2 Corinthians 13:14**, where he speaks of "*the grace of the Lord Jesus **Christ**, the love of **God**, and the fellowship of the **Holy Spirit**.*" Theophilus of Antioch, in the late 2nd century, is one of the first to use the term "Trinity" to describe God's triune nature.[80] Irenaeus (c. 130–202 AD) highlighted the unity of God while recognizing the unique roles of the Father, Son, and Holy Spirit. Tertullian (c. 155–220 AD), the first to use the Latin term *Trinitas*, described God as one substance expressed in three distinct persons.

In 325 AD the now infamous Council of Nicaea, convened by Emperor Constantine, was pivotal in defining the orthodox understanding of the Trinity. The Nicene Creed declared that the Son is "of the same substance" as the Father, affirming their equality and divinity. The creed also affirmed the Holy Spirit, though its role was clarified further in subsequent councils. In 381 AD the First Council of Constantinople expanded on the Nicene Creed and provided a clearer definition of the Holy Spirit's divinity and personhood.[81] This council declared the Holy Spirit to be worshiped and glorified together with the Father and the Son, solidifying the Trinitarian doctrine. This doctrine reflects centuries of theological debate as the church sought to articulate the nature of God's unity and diversity. The resulting doctrine is that God exists as one being in three persons, each fully and equally divine, yet distinct in relation to each other. So, let's explore a few of the early "heresies" the Holy Roman Empire grappled with for a moment.

---

[80] Jaroslav Pelikan, *The Christian Tradition: A History of the Development of Doctrine, Volume 1: The Emergence of the Catholic Tradition* (100-600) (Chicago: University of Chicago Press, 1971), 173-179.
[81] Philip Schaff, *History of the Christian Church, Volume III: Nicene and Post-Nicene Christianity* (Grand Rapids, MI: Eerdmans, 1910), 619-625.

We have already discussed Gnosticism and the concept of "gnosis" throughout this book. Gnostic teachings varied, but many Gnostics believed in a dualistic system where the material world was basically seen as evil and the spiritual realm was the true, pure reality. Jesus, in this view, was considered a purely spiritual being who came to impart hidden knowledge to save those who were spiritually advanced. The orthodox church's response emphasized that Jesus was fully divine and fully human, countering the Gnostic idea that his divinity was separate from or superior to his humanity. The church stressed that God's creation was good, although apparently man was not due to his "sinful" nature, and that Jesus' incarnation in the material world was essential for salvation.

With the creation of the concepts of the Holy Trinity, we can see that the Roman Catholic Church was intent on ensuring that Jesus was seen as equal to God the Father. In doing so they were able to ensure that their religion would reign supreme over all others by definition. It should be quite obvious by now that this was the primary objective of most all decisions that were made by the Holy Roman Empire. However, I would submit to you this was in no way what the Christ Consciousness was teaching us through the words of Jesus. Let us examine several instances when he was obviously saying something different.

John 5:19 - *"Then Jesus answered and said to them, 'Most assuredly, I say to you, the* **Son can do nothing of Himself***, but* **what He sees the Father do***; for whatever He does, the Son also does in like manner.'"* - In this verse we see that Jesus emphasizes his dependence on the Father, indicating that he follows the Father's actions and is not acting independently.

John 5:30 - *"***I can of Myself do nothing***. As I hear, I judge; and My judgment is righteous, because I do not seek My own will but* **the will of the Father** *who sent Me."* - Here, Jesus clarifies that his actions and judgments are directed by the Father's will, not his own.

John 14:28 - *"You have heard Me say to you, 'I am going away and coming back to you.' If you loved Me, you would rejoice because I said, 'I am going to the Father,'* **for My Father is greater than I."** - Here Jesus explicitly states that the Father is greater than himself, suggesting a hierarchical relationship. Does this sound like he thought of himself as equal with God the Father?

John 7:16 - *"Jesus answered them and said,* **'My doctrine is not Mine,** *but* **His who sent Me.**'" - Jesus indicates that his teachings come from the Father, not from his own authority.

John 8:28 - *"Then Jesus said to them, 'When you lift up the Son of Man, then you will know that I am He, and that* **I do nothing of Myself***; but as* **My Father taught Me***, I speak these things.'"* Again, Jesus shows that his teachings and actions are guided by the Father, thus emphasizing the separation as distinct entities.

John 12:49 - *"For I have not spoken on* **My own authority***; but* **the Father who sent Me** *gave Me a command, what I should say and what I should speak."* - Jesus makes it clear that his words come from the Father's command, not his own initiative.

Matthew 26:39 - *"He went a little farther and fell on His face, and prayed, saying, 'O* **My Father***, if it is possible, let this cup pass from Me; nevertheless,* **not as I will, but as You will.**'" - In the Garden of Gethsemane, Jesus submits to the Father's will, showing a distinction between his own desire and the Father's plan.

John 14:10 - *"Do you not believe that I am in the Father, and the Father in Me? The words that I speak to you* **I do not speak on My own authority***; but the* **Father who dwells in Me** *does the works."* - Here Jesus describes a relationship of unity with the Father while still showing that his authority and works come from the Father.

Mark 13:32 - *"But of that day and hour no one knows, not even the angels in heaven,* **nor the Son,** *but only* **the Father***."* - Jesus distinguishes his knowledge from the Father's, indicating that only the

Father knows the timing of the end. If Jesus were truly one and the same with the Father, then would he not also know the day and the hour?

John 6:38 - *"For I have come down from heaven, not to do **My own will**, but the will of **Him who sent Me**."* - This verse emphasizes that Jesus's mission was to carry out the Father's will, not his own.

Does it not seem clear that Jesus did not consider himself to be the same as, or equal to, God the Father? Then why would those who follow His teachings do so? I would submit to you that if Jesus were standing before us today, he would consider most of what the Holy Roman Empire said about him to be more blasphemous than anything the Pharisees ever directly accused of Him. As in most cases, to justify this stance one must do a fair amount of manipulation of concepts.

When Jesus was instructing us to baptize in the name of the Father, and the Son, and the Holy Spirit, he was telling us that all three were part of the same whole in spirit, just as we all are a part of the **ONE** Universal Consciousness that is the Father. When Jesus said in **John 14:20**, "*At that day ye shall know that **I am in my Father**, and **ye in me**, and **I in you***", he was explaining that he was in a state of Christ Consciousness, where his will was to do that of the Father's. The Christos can and will deliver all things to you through the Holy Spirit dwelling inside you. For he said, "*whoever believes in me **will do the works I have been doing**, and they **will do even greater things** than these*",

Now, I am not insinuating that there is no hierarchy of spiritual beings, for surely there are entities who are much farther advanced spiritually than us. There have been many ascended masters who have sacrificed their energy to help humanity advance farther, and I in no way consider myself worthy to be considered at their level in any sense. However, ultimately, we all are born of the same spiritual energetic essence in the Quantum Field which is the **ONE**, the Father. By accepting Christ Consciousness into your own field of being, you will be able to do the things that Jesus did, and in doing so you will become one who was spoken of, *"I said, 'You are "gods"; **you are all sons of the Most High.**'"*

The Trinity of Consciousness

To fully comprehend the guidance of the Spirit, one must embrace a framework I describe as "The Trinity of Consciousness." For this is the only way that you can comprehend the things of the Spirit. It is something we talked about in the first chapter of this book, and now that we have come full circle, I would like to cover this concept again in a slightly different light. It is the concept of Heart-Brain Coherence and Living from a balanced perspective. Previously, we explored the distinct functions of the brain's hemispheres: the analytical Left-Brain (intellect) and the intuitive Right-Brain (gnosis). Achieving harmony between these aspects is essential so that you can begin to "Feel" and "Know" truth. What sits exactly between those two hemispheres positioned perfectly in the middle? The Pineal Gland...

Referred to as the "Third Eye" in spiritual traditions, the pineal gland exhibits structural features remarkably akin to those of the eyes. This small, pinecone-shaped endocrine gland is located in the center of the brain, and it plays a crucial role in regulating circadian rhythms by producing the hormone melatonin.[82] The physical similarities between the pineal gland and the eyes are not merely metaphorical; they extend to anatomical features as well. One of the most striking similarities is the presence of cells within the pineal gland that are comparable to the photoreceptor cells found in the retina of the eyes. These pinealocytes are specialized cells that have light-sensitive properties, akin to the rods and cones in the retina that detect light and send signals to the brain.

Additionally, the pineal gland is connected to the visual pathway through a structure called the retinohypothalamic tract. This connection allows the gland to receive information about light and dark cycles from the eyes, which influences melatonin secretion. In some ancient

---

[82] Rick Strassman, *DMT: The Spirit Molecule* (Rochester, VT: Park Street Press, 2001), 60-65.

vertebrates, the pineal gland even served as a light-sensing organ, similar to an eye. The gland's resemblance to an eye is further emphasized by its ability to respond to light and its development from the same embryonic tissue layer that forms the eyes. These similarities have contributed to the pineal gland's reputation as a "spiritual eye," with various cultural and esoteric traditions associating it with higher states of awareness, intuition, and consciousness.

The pineal gland, sometimes referred to as the "seat of the soul," contains tiny crystalline structures composed primarily of calcium phosphate and calcium carbonate. What makes these crystals particularly interesting is their potential piezoelectric properties. This is significant because it has led some researchers to suggest that the pineal gland's crystalline structures could play a role in bioelectrical communication or in sensing electromagnetic fields. Although we have somewhat discussed electromagnetic fields in this book, it will be covered more in depth in our next book. Suffice it to say that electromagnetic fields are where the true spiritual resonance is felt.

The piezoelectric effect of these crystals may help explain why the pineal gland has been associated with spiritual experiences, and altered states of consciousness. Thus, the activation of the pineal gland can lead to heightened awareness, intuition, and even perception of higher dimensions. The concept that these crystals could respond to subtle changes in electromagnetic fields provides a scientific angle to the esoteric idea of the pineal gland as the "third eye."

It is also believed that the pineal gland may be involved in the production of dimethyltryptamine (DMT) within the brain.[83] DMT is quite possibly the most powerful psychoactive compound on the planet, yet it is found in many plants and animals, including humans. Ingesting DMT creates a profound spiritual, even multi-dimensional experience which leaves one with a completely different perspective

---

[83] Rick Strassman, *DMT: The Spirit Molecule* (Rochester, VT: Park Street Press, 2001), 75-80.

on life and the cosmos. The notion that the pineal gland, or "Third Eye", is involved in the production of DMT, as well as increasing the perception of electromagnetic field energies, means that it is a very important facet to the awakening of consciousness.

We are now coming to an age when the Right-Brain Gnosis is coming back online again, and it is going to shift our entire reality, because with the Right-Brain approach you simply "Know" Truth experientially, rather than needing hard physical evidence of it, which is what the Left-Brain requires before it can fully accept something as Truth. So, we must learn to approach life from a more balanced approach, and when we do this the pineal gland will start to come online more actively supporting the spiritual awakening process.

The concept of Heart-Brain Coherence integrates emotional energy into our understanding of the body's interconnected systems. Emotional energy represents one of the most potent aspects of human existence, as its bioelectromagnetic field interacts profoundly with the Quantum Field, and thus it has a direct effect on the local field in which you are immersed. That "Field" is where Quantum Physics tells us EVERYTHING comes from. In my current intuitive understanding, or gnosis, the Quantum Field is the energetic field of Universal Consciousness (i.e. - The Mind of God).

Medical Science has now shown that the Heart is really the most powerful organ in the body[84], not the brain. The Heart emits what is by far the most powerful electromagnetic field in the body, which can now be measured scientifically. The heart also has its own internal "brain", if you will, made up of the same type of neurons as are found in the brain. The Heart sends twice as many signals to the brain, as the brain does the heart, so we can safely assume that the Heart most likely has more influence over your conscious experience than the brain.

---

[84] Rollin McCraty, *The Energetic Heart: Bioelectromagnetic Interactions Within and Between People* (Boulder Creek, CA: HeartMath Institute, 2015), 20-25.

Nikola Tesla once remarked, *"If your **hate** could be turned into **electricity**, it would **light up the whole world**,"* emphasizing the immense energy tied to human emotions.

The heart is universally recognized as the center of emotional experience, emitting the strongest electromagnetic field in the human body. Then we can surmise that our emotional energy emits the strongest energetic waves into our local field. This is why your emotional state can have such a strong impact on those around you, and vice-versa. Just think about the metaphor of the waves that flow out from your movement in a calm pool of water. They travel until they hit something solid like the wall of the pool, and then they bounce back to you. The exact same thing happens with regards to the electromagnetic waves you emit from your emotional energies through the heart. Thus, anyone near you will be bombarded by the emotional waves you are emitting. Then, that person will most likely automatically reflect the same type of waves back to you. Therefore, in a very real sense, you have a direct impact on not only those around you, but also on the energetic reality that you create for yourself. This is why it is so important to put out positive emotions and energy in every situation.

If you take them all together in a metaphorical sense you really have the True Trinity of God! Left-Brain (Intellect), Right-Brain (Spirit), and the Heart (Creator of Energy). In this context it lines up in this symbolic framework:

- The Father aligns with the Heart, the source of creative energy.
- The Son corresponds to the Left-Brain, representing intellect and logic.
- The Holy Spirit reflects the Right-Brain, embodying intuition and spiritual connection.

So, the next time you hear someone talk about the "Trinity" you should have a much more holistic and balanced concept from which to contemplate their words. Then you will be able to take this conceptual understanding and apply it to the very actions you take within your life, and your interactions with those around you. Consciously realizing these simple truths will impact your field of reality, and thus the fields of those with which you live. This will allow you to be an active participant in bringing heaven to earth.

As we reflect on the threefold path of consciousness: Victim, Creator, and Unity; we come face to face with the central gatekeeper on this journey: the ego. It is the ego that clings to the illusion of separation, feeding the false identities that keep us bound to fear and suffering. And yet, the ego itself is not to be hated or destroyed, it is to be understood, integrated, and transcended. What follows is a deeper look at how the ego became the archetype of the Beast and how its loving transformation opens the door to Christ Consciousness.

The Ego, the Beast, and the Death of Separation

One of the greatest misunderstandings in modern spirituality is the belief that the ego must be violently conquered or destroyed. But Christ Consciousness reveals something more profound: the ego is not the enemy, it is the illusion of separation. It is the shadow we must understand, not the demon we must destroy.

In the Book of Revelation, the Beast is described as a force of domination, deception, and control. But what if the Beast is not merely some future tyrant, but a symbolic representation of the egoic mind? The ego, the small self rooted in fear and division, is the very Beast that rules the inner world of the unawakened soul. It thrives on judgment, pride, shame, and the need to control or be superior.

Yet the ego, as problematic as it can become, was a necessary stage in our spiritual evolution. It arises from the most basic animal instinct for survival, and it gives us the experience of individuality, of being a distinct "self" navigating through a world of others. Without the ego, we could not develop self-awareness or personal agency. It is the vehicle through which consciousness enters into separation so that it may eventually return to unity with deeper understanding.

Christ did not come to wage war against the ego through force or condemnation. He came to illuminate it through love. The true path is not to kill the ego, but to lovingly integrate it. To see through its illusions and return to the wholeness of being. The death of self that

Christ speaks of is the death of the ego's rule over the soul, not the destruction of individuality.

This is why the Tarot's Death card, which many associate with fear, is actually a symbol of transformation. It marks the end of egoic control and the rebirth of the authentic Self, the divine essence within. Christ's message was not one of violence, but of transcendence. *"Whoever loses their life for my sake will find it"* (**Matthew 10:39**) is not a call to physical martyrdom, but to egoic surrender.

When we stop identifying with the voice of fear, and begin to embody the voice of love, the ego is no longer in control. It becomes what it was meant to be: a tool for navigating this world, not just a tyrant ruling it.

Christ Consciousness invites us not to fight the Beast, but to see through it. And in doing so, we realize that the only thing that ever needed to die…was the illusion of separation.

The Gospel of Paul: A Message Tainted by Ego

The contrast between the teachings of Jesus and the theology promoted by Paul becomes even more striking when we consider the role of the ego. While Christ taught radical humility, forgiveness, and inner transformation, Paul's letters often center around obedience, sin, judgment, and exclusion. This shift is not accidental. It reflects the unresolved egoic wounds Paul carried with him.

Paul, by his own admission, was haunted by his past. Once a persecutor of the early followers of The Way, his dramatic conversion experience on the road to Damascus created a psychological fracture that seems to have influenced his writings. His gospel, though wrapped in language of grace, still leans heavily on fear, submission, and hierarchy. In contrast to Jesus' invitation to become **One with the Divine**, Paul paints a picture of a distant, wrathful God whose favor can only be earned through proper belief.

Throughout Paul's letters, we also find repeated references to his own status and authority. He often defends himself, asserts his apostleship, and distances himself from the original disciples. Unlike Jesus, who consistently deflected attention away from himself and pointed toward the Father within, Paul's message centers more on himself and his version of the gospel.

Many scholars have noted that the Gospel of John, written decades after the synoptic gospels and long after Paul's influence had spread, reflects theological ideas much more closely aligned with Paul's message than with the original teachings of Christ. This suggests that as the church began to consolidate power, Paul's ego-driven framework became the theological foundation, while the spiritual message of Christ Consciousness was pushed aside.

This is not to demonize Paul, but to understand him. His struggle was the same as all of ours: the tension between the ego and the soul. But when his writings are taken as doctrine over the direct words of Jesus, the result is a faith built on fear rather than love, obedience rather than freedom, and separation rather than union.

True Christ Consciousness offers something far greater: the realization that the **Kingdom is within**, that God is not a distant ruler but the very Source of our being, and that we are all invited to awaken, not through fear, but through Love.

The Return to Oneness

The journey into Christ Consciousness is not a climb up a mountain to reach God. It is a return inward to the place where God has always dwelled: within. It is not about adding more knowledge or religious rituals, but about removing the veils that have blinded us to our own divinity.

Through understanding the ego, not as a villain but as a necessary stage in our evolution, we reclaim our power to choose love over fear, unity over separation. Through seeing past the distortions of Pauline doctrine, we rediscover the living message of Christ, who came not to start a new religion but to awaken humanity to its inherent divine nature.

This is the essence of Christ Consciousness: not worshiping Christ from afar, but embodying the same frequency of unconditional love that He lived. It is the realization that we, too, are the light of the world. That we, too, are the temple where Spirit dwells. That we, too, are called to rise, not in pride, but in presence.

As we awaken to this truth, the veil begins to lift. The Kingdom is revealed. And the long exile from our Source comes to an end, not because God moved, but because we finally remembered who we are and where He was the whole time.

Chapter-9: The Power of Prayer

Across various spiritual traditions, prayer is described as a powerful practice capable of achieving the extraordinary, but why is this so? Does prayer possess a unique quality that genuinely impacts practitioners' lives? The short answer is yes, though the full explanation is more nuanced.

Prayer, at its core, is a practice of aligning with the Divine, whether by requesting guidance or interceding on behalf of another. While the specifics of prayer vary across religious traditions, at its core, it often centers on seeking assistance or blessings. In contemporary spirituality, prayer is frequently understood as an affirmation of intention, aligning the self with universal energies. It is a way to put one's self in alignment with the Universe, in order to manifest desires or healing.

Many left-brain-oriented materialists dismiss prayer as futile, often questioning, "If prayer and God are so powerful, why do hardships still occur?" As if the barrier to reality is that only good things will happen if "God" is "Real". Yet, this perspective overlooks the complexities of how the universe operates. If reincarnation holds true, as several pieces of evidence suggest which we will again cover in-depth in our next book, then our souls return to the material realm multiple times. So, why would you choose to incarnate here at all? The apparent purpose is to experience life, but given its inherent challenges, one might still wonder…why?

Many spiritual traditions affirm that reincarnation allows souls to evolve and attain spiritual growth. If you think back honestly upon your life, then you will most likely acknowledge that you did not grow the most during the good times, but rather it was the struggles in life that pushed you to become the best version of yourself. As my late sensei used to always say, "**Pain is the greatest Teacher…**" The older I get the more I realize the absolute truth in that statement. When things cause you pain you are more motivated to make a change! Thus, if our goal was truly to grow, then we would not choose an easy life, but a more difficult one that would challenge us in ways we have not been challenged before. In that regard, it is a blessing to go through pain and personal tribulation.

James 1:2-4 (NIRV) - "*My brothers and sisters,* **you will face all kinds of trouble***. When you do,* **think of it as pure joy***. Your faith will be tested. You know that when this happens* **it will produce in you the strength to continue***. And you must allow this strength to finish its work.* **Then you will be all you should be***. You will have everything you need..*"

This passage encourages believers to embrace trials as opportunities for spiritual growth, reinforcing the idea that challenges refine character and deepen faith. Thus, it is really all about the perspective one chooses to adopt about the difficulties faced in life! So, choose to have a grateful heart no matter what situation you find yourself in.

A Personal Experience

Allow me to share a deeply personal account that highlights the profound impact prayer has had in my life. On Memorial day in the year 2000 my son was born three months premature, and he only weighed about 2-pounds 8-ounces at birth. Thus, he had to spend the first month of his life in the Neonatal Intensive Care Unit, otherwise known as the NICU. A baby develops their immune system in the last trimester of the pregnancy, so when they are born three months premature they have virtually no immunity to anything. Thus they are very susceptible to all types of infection.

At about two weeks old, I got a dreaded phone call at work from the hospital late one afternoon. They told me my son had contracted NICS, or NeonatalIntensive Care Sepsis, which is a life-threatening infection that enters the bloodstream and overwhelms the premature infant's immune system. I was told the situation was serious and I needed to get to the hospital as quickly as possible! However, before I left work I sat down at my desk and said a prayer asking for healing for my baby boy. It was at that very moment, as I was finishing up the prayer, that I heard a small still voice in my head tell me that he was going to be okay. My crown chakra lit up like a christmas tree, which I had already learned was "the Spirit" speaking validation to me through the electromagnetic field. So, I drove to the hospital fully confident that my son was going to be okay.

However, when I arrived at the NICU, I found my wife and parents off to the side crying, and the doctor and nurses could barely look me in the eye. I walked up to my sobbing wife and told her that everything was going to be okay, that I had prayed and was told he was going to be okay. At that moment a nurse grabbed me by the arm and pulled me to the side. She very brashly said that I didn't need to be putting a false sense of hope in my wife's heart, because my child had less than a 10% chance of even making it through the night. I replied to her, "Look, I'm sorry, but I prayed, and I was told that he was going to be okay." The nurse just shook her head, and walked away in total disbelief.

It was then that I turned to really see my son for the first time. He was on a bright white table in the middle of the room, and absolutely no one was standing near to him. Everyone in the room had their backs turned to him, because they could not bear to look at him, and I quickly understood why. He was absolutely pale white with no color, and no sign of life whatsoever. The only movement was from the vibrating table, which was the only thing keeping air in his lungs, and thus keeping him alive at that point. He honestly looked like he was already dead…

I walked up to the table and stood next to him, and began to pray in the best way I knew how. I prayed, "Father I come to you in the name of Jesus Christ asking you to heal my son in a miraculous and powerful way. **Christos Domini!**" This was a phrase that I had been given by Spirit, at that point in time, to close all my prayers with. I did not even know what the words meant at the time, but I knew they held power! It was at that moment, when I felt what I can only describe as a beam of energy shoot down through the ceiling onto my son's lifeless body. It was so powerful that it made my crown chakra light up like a christmas tree, and all the hair stood up on my entire body! I was the only person close to him when this happened, and I instantly knew that he was being healed, at that very moment! As I stood there with tears rolling down my cheeks, I thanked God for the miraculous healing that was taking place in his body, as if it was already a done deal. It was immediately after this the doctor told us it was way past visiting hours so we had to leave. I gathered my sobbing wife, and we went home for the night.

The next morning, we were awakened by the phone ringing sharply at 8:00 AM, and it was the doctor who said we needed to come back down to the hospital immediately! At this point, I honestly lost my faith momentarily, as I thought he was calling us because our son was dying, and he wanted to give us one last chance to say goodbye. I drove us to the hospital expecting the worst. I think my wife and I both cried silently all the way to the hospital.

I can remember walking up to the double metal doors at the entryway to the NICU, and the doctor excitedly burst through the doors with a look of amazement on his face smiling from ear to ear! He said to us, "Guys in my twenty years in medical practice, this is the first honest-to-God miracle that I have ever witnessed! Your son should be dead right now, but he has completely turned around! He has his color back and he is breathing on his own, and we cannot find any trace of the infection in him! We have even fed him once already this morning! This should not have happened…"

My wife and I both instantly burst into tears of joy! As we excitedly walked into the room to see our completely healthy little baby boy, the nurse from the previous night stopped me with tears in her eyes. She said, "I am so sorry for what I said to you last night…I just did not know?" I told her that it was perfectly okay, and that I would have probably felt the same way, had I been in her shoes. She just smiled and hugged me.

This was my first major lesson in the power of Prayer, but what spirit showed me was that it was my absolute Faith in the face of total despair that was the catalyst for the healing! It was then when I was reminded of the following times when Yeshua had healed someone, and then emphasized that it was their **Faith** that healed them.

In the book of Mark, there is the story of a blind man named Bartimaeus, who called out to Jesus for mercy as he passed by. When Jesus asked him what he wanted he replied, "*Lord, I want to see.*" Jesus responded: "*Go, **your faith has healed you**.*" Immediately, Bartimaeus received his sight and followed Jesus. - **Mark 10:52**

In the book of Luke there is a story of Jesus healing ten men, who suffered from Leprosy, but only one of them returned to thank him. Jesus then said to the man who returned: "*Rise and go; **your faith has made you well**.*" - **Luke 17:19**

Again in the book of Luke, there is a story of a woman, who is described as sinful, who anointed the feet of Jesus with perfume and tears. Jesus acknowledged her love and repentance, and forgave her sins, telling her: "***Your faith has saved you**; go in peace.*" - **Luke 7:50**

Then in the book of Matthew there is the story of the Roman centurion who came to Jesus, and asked him to heal his servant. The centurion showed an extraordinary level of Faith by saying that Jesus only needed to speak the word, and his servant would be healed. Jesus marveled at his faith and said: "*Go! Let it be done just **as you believed it would**.*" - **Matthew 8:13**

In all four of these examples, it was the act of Faith of the individual that was the catalyst for the miracle, just as the Spirit told me that it was my Faith in my son's healing, when all others wavered, which was the catalyst for his miraculous recovery. You see, it is the emotions that you "**feel**" through **Faith** in the moment of tribulation which releases the positive electromagnetic energy from your **Heart** into the **Field** which causes the miracle to happen! For as the observer effect shows us in quantum mechanics, consciousness has a direct impact on the quantum field. Thus, you can and do have a direct impact on the world around you by the way you interact with the field. More on this in the next book!

From that day on, I have never forgotten that lesson, and it is something I carry with me to this day. I am literally weeping with tears right now as I type these words, because the events of that day still have such a powerful impact on my spirit. I cannot tell that story without tearing up...

The Lord's Prayer

The Lord's Prayer, one of the most central prayers in Christianity, was originally spoken by Jesus in Aramaic, the language of his people. While the prayer is widely known today in its Greek and later English translations, the nuances and depth of meaning in Aramaic offer a far more expansive understanding of its original intent. This is due to the fact that Aramaic, like other Semitic languages, has a rich and multi-layered nature. Words often carry multiple meanings, blending the physical, spiritual, and emotional realms. This allows for more symbolic and poetic interpretations, where a single phrase can invoke both immediate and eternal truths.

In the case of the Lord's Prayer, what we often read in English as simple supplication in, "*Our Father who art in heaven*" or "*Give us this day our daily bread*", carries far deeper connotations in Aramaic. The language invites a mystical reading, where the prayer becomes not just a list of requests, but a profound statement of the human relationship with the Divine, the cosmos, and each other.[85]

When Jesus said, "*Abwoon d'bashmaya,*" the first phrase of the prayer, the Aramaic Abwoon is far richer than the simple "Father" found in English translations. In Aramaic, Abwoon evokes both masculine and feminine aspects of the divine. It's a term that implies a cosmic parent, or the source of all creation, nurturing yet powerful, transcending the limitations of gender. This word sets the tone for the entire prayer, as it is not merely addressed to a paternal figure, but to the source of all life.

---

[85] Neil Douglas-Klotz, *Prayers of the Cosmos: Meditations on the Aramaic Words of Jesus* (San Francisco: HarperOne, 1990), 19-27.

"*Nethqadash shmakh*" was translated as "*Hallowed be thy name*", but in Aramaic it expresses more than just a reverence for God's name. It suggests that the divine name itself is to shine forth, becoming holy through the actions and awareness of the one praying. It's not a passive declaration; it's an invocation for God's name to be sanctified in the world through human consciousness and actions.

The phrase "*Teytey malkuthakh*," or "*Thy kingdom come*," in Aramaic carries a profound, spiritual meaning. Malkuthakh, which means "kingdom," can also refer to divine sovereignty or God's reign, not only in an eschatological sense, but within us and around us, in the present moment. It emphasizes the prayer as a call to action, to bring about a world in alignment with divine will.

"*Nehwey tzevyanach*", translated as "*Thy will be done*", in Aramaic is more about harmonizing with the flow of divine purpose. It implies that our role as human beings is to align ourselves with the divine plan. It's an invitation to act in accordance with cosmic harmony rather than merely submitting to it. In Aramaic, this idea blends with the imagery of the natural world, suggesting that just as the stars and planets follow their divine courses, so too should we seek to move in accord with that same will.

When we arrive at "*Hawvlan lachma d'sunqanan yaomana*," or "*Give us this day our daily bread*," the Aramaic term lachma can be understood not just as physical sustenance, but as spiritual nourishment. In this context, the prayer asks for what is necessary not only to feed the body but also to sustain the spirit, as the bread of life that nourishes the soul.

"*Washboqlan khaubayn*", translated as "*Forgive us our debts*", is another phrase layered with meaning. In Aramaic, the word khaubayn can refer to sins, offenses, or moral failings, but it also carries a more literal meaning of debts. This brings the moral and the material into harmony, asking for forgiveness in both a spiritual sense, or our wrongdoings, and a practical sense to forgiveness of obligations.

Neil Douglas-Klotz, a scholar of Aramaic and Sufi mysticism, offers a poetic and mystical interpretation of the Lord's Prayer, deeply connected to the nuances of Aramaic. His translation opens a door to experience the prayer as a cosmic invocation, one that harmonizes inner and outer worlds. Douglas-Klotz emphasizes that the prayer is not simply a list of supplications, but a dynamic invitation to align with the creative forces of the universe.

Here is Neil Douglas-Klotz interpretation with elaboration[86]:
"O cosmic Birther of all radiance and vibration, soften the ground of our being and carve out a space within us where Your Presence can abide."

This first line reflects the vibrational nature of the universe. Douglas-Klotz highlights the concept that the divine, like a birthing force, emanates through all levels of existence as vibration. Here there is similarity to the concepts we see today in Quantum Field Theory, which I will cover in-depth in the next book. Douglas-Klotz views the opening of the prayer as an invitation for divine energy to penetrate the human spirit, softening the ego and opening space for divine presence to dwell within.

"Fill us with Your creativity so that we may be empowered to bear the fruit of Your mission."

This line touches on the idea that the divine spirit infuses us with creativity and purpose. Rather than merely asking for earthly sustenance alone, we ask to become vessels of divine creativity, capable of manifesting what is in harmony with the divine will. *"Not my will, but your will be done..."*

"Let each of our actions bear fruit in accordance with Your desire."

---

[86] Neil Douglas-Klotz, Prayers of the Cosmos: Meditations on the Aramaic Words of Jesus (San Francisco: HarperOne, 1990), 29-38.

Douglas-Klotz's interpretation suggests that our actions are expressions of divine will, reflecting the Aramaic view that divine and human purposes are intertwined. In essence, we are co-creators with the divine, and our lives should be an expression of this harmony.

"Untie the tangled threads of destiny that bind us, as we release others from the entanglement of past mistakes."

The phrase traditionally rendered as *"forgive us our debts as we forgive our debtors"* is here expanded to reflect the interconnected nature of life. Douglas-Klotz focuses on the image of untangling, thus releasing both ourselves and others from the knots of past errors. In this view, forgiveness is not just about moral absolution, but a liberation from the bonds of karma or fate that keep us trapped in cycles of guilt and retribution.

"Do not let us be seduced by that which would divert us from our true purpose, but illuminate the opportunities of the present moment."

This interpretation transforms *"lead us not into temptation"* into a call for mindfulness and awareness. It asks for clarity to recognize distractions from our spiritual path, and to see the divine opportunities presented in each moment.

"For You are the ground and the fruitful vision, the birth-power and fulfillment, as all is gathered and made whole once again."

The closing lines shift the focus from abstract power to wholeness and unity. They emphasize the divine as the foundation of all life, the source from which everything arises, and the force that gathers all creation back into a harmonious whole.

The Aramaic version of the Lord's Prayer invites a deeper, more mystical connection with the divine. Through this lens, the prayer is not just a request for material needs or moral guidance, but a profound expression of the cosmic relationship between the human soul and the divine creator. Neil Douglas-Klotz's poetic rendering brings this vision to life, transforming the prayer into a vibrational dialogue between humanity and the universe. In this light, the Lord's Prayer is not merely a relic of Christian tradition, but a living invocation of divine energy, reminding us of our interconnectedness with all creation, and our role as co-creators in the unfolding of divine will.

Chapter-10: The Importance of Meditation

The practice of meditation is one of the most important facets of most Eastern spiritual philosophies, but many in the West do not fully grasp what meditation is, and why it is so important. So, let us now examine some of the primary philosophies surrounding meditation, and uncover what makes it so powerful.

The Buddha's core teachings on meditation revolve around mindfulness, as a way to develop insight into the true nature of reality. Meditation is not just about calming the mind, but about gaining wisdom by observing the impermanent and interconnected nature of thoughts, feelings, and the world. One of his core sayings on meditation was, "*Just as a snake sheds its skin, we must shed our past over and over again.*" This metaphor highlights how mindfulness and meditation allow us to release attachments, and stay present in the moment, fostering personal transformation.[87] It also reminds us that we must daily evaluate the actions and feelings felt, and forgive ourselves and others in order to release the negative energies.

In the *Bhagavad Gita*, Lord Krishna speaks to Arjuna about the importance of Dhyana Yoga, the path of meditation, to attain inner peace and union with the divine. He emphasizes that true meditation leads to a state of equanimity and mental stillness. He once said, "When meditation is mastered, the mind is unwavering like the flame of a lamp in a windless place." This describes the inner calm and focus that meditation cultivates, creating a deep connection between the individual and the universal consciousness.[88]

Taoism teaches that sitting meditation, called **Zuowang**, translates to "*sitting and forgetting.*" It is essential to align with the Tao, which means "***The Way***," the ultimate reality or universal flow. This

---

[87] Thich Nhat Hanh, *The Heart of the Buddha's Teaching: Transforming Suffering into Peace, Joy, and Liberation* (New York: Broadway Books, 1998), 89-94.
[88] Eknath Easwaran, *The Bhagavad Gita* (Tomales, CA: Nilgiri Press, 2007), 122-126.

philosophy can be summed up in the parable of the "River of Life," which states that life is like a river. You can fight against the current, to try to get to where you think you need to go, or you can let go and allow the river to take you where you were intended to be. The purpose of Taoist meditation is to empty the mind, and dissolve into the natural state of non-action, allowing wisdom to arise spontaneously. Lao Tzu once said, *"To the mind that is still, the whole universe surrenders."* This highlights how meditation can lead to profound understanding and unity with the cosmos, through stillness.[89]

Patanjali's *Yoga Sutras* outline meditation as a key step toward Samadhi, a state of meditative absorption, where the self merges with the object of meditation. This leads to profound peace and spiritual liberation, for *"Meditation is the continuous flow of consciousness toward an object."* This teaching emphasizes that through consistent practice, one transcends the duality between the self and the object of focus, resulting in deep unity with the divine.

Sufi mystics practice Dhikr, a form of meditative repetition of God's name, to reach deeper states of spiritual awareness. It helps practitioners transcend the ego and attain unity with the divine. Rumi once said, *"Listen to the silence. It has so much to say."* This reflects the deep state of meditative awareness cultivated through Dhikr, where one goes beyond words, into the silence where divine truth is experienced.[90]

In Kabbalistic practice, meditation (Hitbonenut) is a way to connect with the divine energy of God. Through visualization, prayer, and focus, Kabbalists believe meditation allows one to ascend spiritually and experience divine wisdom. It is said, *"When you are in meditation, ascend higher and higher... until the soul sheds the corporeal senses and the divine light is revealed."* This teaching emphasizes using

---

[89] Lao Tzu, *Tao Te Ching*, trans. Stephen Mitchell (New York: Harper & Row, 1988), 56-59.

[90] Jalaluddin Rumi, *The Essential Rumi*, trans. Coleman Barks (San Francisco: HarperOne, 1995), 114-118.

meditation as a gateway to higher spiritual realms and divine knowledge.[91]

Each of these teachings emphasizes a slightly different path, but they all converge on the idea that meditation is a powerful tool for inner transformation, peace, and communion with a higher reality. Although traditional Christian prayer focuses primarily on supplication, contemplative prayer, as a meditative practice, was central to early Christian mystics. This type of prayer involves silent communion with God and meditation on divine truths. Contemplative meditation encourages individuals to focus inwardly, seeking divine presence and wisdom within themselves rather than externally, because, "**The kingdom of God is within you.**"

I have encountered many Christians who think that meditation and breathwork are practices that invite evil spirits to possess the practitioner. However, I can assure you from my own personal experience that nothing could be further from the truth. This idea was injected into Catholic doctrine by the Empire, because they did not want people to practice meditation. For the Empire knew that if they did, individuals would soon come to understand that they did not need a priest to intercede for them, and the "The Church" would lose its grip on power. Once again, we find that what the Roman "Church" propagates had absolutely nothing to do with what Yeshua actually did and taught. Here are some examples to highlight this point.

Before beginning his public ministry, Jesus spent 40 days alone in the wilderness, fasting and meditating. This period of intense solitude and prayer prepared him for the spiritual challenges ahead. *"Then Jesus was led by the Spirit into the wilderness to be tempted by the devil.* ***After fasting forty days and forty nights****, he was hungry."* – **Matthew 4:1-2**.

Before choosing the twelve apostles, Jesus spent the entire night alone in prayer on a mountainside, showing the importance of

---

[91] Aryeh Kaplan, *Meditation and Kabbalah* (York Beach, ME: Weiser Books, 1982), 45-52.

meditation before making important decisions. *"One of those days Jesus went out to a mountainside to pray, and* **spent the night praying to God."** – **Luke 6:12**.

After feeding the 5,000, Jesus retreated to a mountainside to pray in solitude, showing the importance of private meditation and prayer. *"After he had dismissed them,* **he went up on a mountainside by himself to pray**. *Later that night, he was there alone."* – **Matthew 14:23**.

Another instance in Mark records Jesus going alone to the mountainside to pray, indicating his practice of meditation and communion with God following significant events. *"After leaving them,* **he went up on a mountainside to pray**.*"* – **Mark 6:46**.

After healing many people in Capernaum, Jesus rose early and went to a secluded place to pray. This demonstrates his need for quiet reflection, even amidst his busy ministry. *"Very early in the morning, while it was still dark,* **Jesus got up**, *left the house* **and went off to a solitary place, where he prayed**.*"* – **Mark 1:35**.

The following verse reveals that it was a common practice for Jesus to withdraw to solitary places to pray and meditate, especially after performing miracles or during times of decision-making. *"But* **Jesus often withdrew to lonely places and prayed**.*"* – **Luke 5:16**.

Jesus frequently prayed in private, even when his disciples were near. This verse highlights his regular practice of private meditation and prayer. *"***Once when Jesus was praying in private** *and his disciples were with him, he asked them, 'Who do the crowds say I am?'"* – **Luke 9:18**.

On the night of his betrayal, Jesus went to the Garden of Gethsemane to pray alone. This is a powerful example of Jesus seeking deep solitude in the face of immense trials, showing that even the Christ needed meditation to help calm his heart and mind. *"Then Jesus went with his disciples to a place called Gethsemane, and he said to them, 'Sit here* **while I go over there and pray**.*'"* – **Matthew 26:36**.

During the agony in Gethsemane, Jesus withdrew from his disciples to pray alone, showing his intense reliance on solitary prayer in times of great need. *"**He withdrew about a stone's throw beyond them**, knelt down, and prayed."* – **Luke 22:41**.

Similar to **Matthew 26**, this passage emphasizes Jesus' need for solitude in prayer during a time of deep emotional distress. *"They went to a place called Gethsemane, and Jesus said to his disciples, '**Sit here while I pray.**' He took Peter, James, and John along with him, and he began to be deeply distressed and troubled."* – **Mark 14:32-34**.

Finally, the very words purportedly spoken by God himself in **Psalm 45:10** were, "*He says, '**Be still, and know that I am God;**'"* This is describing **EXACTLY** what meditation is and does! When you still your body and mind, then you will find God in that still small voice. In His own words you must first "***Be still***", and then you will know that, "***I AM God.***"

Though it is not explicitly called meditation, this is clearly what Jesus was doing. At its core, meditation is simply about silencing the constant noise in our head that we hear all day long. Ironically, most people in the West have never truly experienced this, because our days are filled with the chatter of smartphones, laptops, televisions, and radios. It's no wonder that mental illness and psychological issues are so rampant in our culture. If you could just let go of all the noise and retreat to a place of solitude, experiencing the bliss of stillness, you would be forever changed.

I'm not saying that you need to become a Buddhist monk, far from it! Nor do you need to spend 3 hours a day in a closet seeking spiritual experiences, though I certainly wouldn't knock that idea at all. All you need to do is take baby steps, and it's easier than you might think. Today, there are many tools to aid you in your journey toward awareness, through still contemplation of your own internal divine spark. Let me tell you about some things I have found useful in my personal journey.

The most important tool I use is sound frequency and vibration. Vibration is the core of our entire reality, and science is just now realizing this truth, again through the concepts in Quantum Field Theory. I will cover this concept extensively in a future book, but suffice it to say that everything in this material world is nothing more than focused vibrational frequency. I have YouTube playlists of my favorite meditational tracks that quickly bring me to a state of relaxation and meditation. You can search for tags like #SolfeggioHealingMusic, #ChakraHealingMusic, or #MeditationMusic and find plenty of options. Once you know what works for you, search for specific frequencies. My personal favorites are 111Hz, 432Hz, and 963Hz, but you should try different tracks until you find the ones that resonate with you. You'll know when you've found them because they will strike a chord of resonance deep within you.

Another thing I find helpful is having a flame nearby if possible. This could be a fire pit outside under the stars, or a candle on the table in front of you. Ideally, you want to be within 3 or 4 feet from the flame, so your electromagnetic field passes through it. Your heart chakra emits the strongest field in your body, known to extend at least 3 feet in all directions. This field is measurable with devices like magnetometers, and some esoteric teachings suggest it can extend 15-20 feet in higher states of expansion. By passing your electromagnetic field through the flame, you cleanse your body's energy, as fire has a purifying effect. Both fire and water have cleansing properties, so trying this exercise in a warm bath with candles would be even more effective!

The most fundamental part of any meditation regimen is learning to focus on the Breath of Life. This is not some esoteric mystery school initiation. I'm talking about simply focusing on your own breathing. That's really it! Breathing is something we do all day, every day, but we take it for granted. Learning to really focus on your breathing is the key to opening the door to meditation. Once you open this door, I promise you will never be the same again. It will change your entire world!

Here's a breathing exercise practice I used years ago to teach me how to breathe. I know, it sounds silly, the idea that you need to learn how to breathe, but you really do because we've been doing it on autopilot for so long that we've forgotten how it should actually be done. This practice will get you on your way faster than anything else I've tried. It's called **21-Breaths**.

First, find a place with no distractions. This could be a natural setting like a forest or garden, or it could simply be your bedroom with the door closed. The more solitude you have, the easier it will be. If you are in your room, try playing one of the meditation tracks you found earlier. Once you have a relaxing set and setting, either sit in a comfortable position, or lie down on your back. It's best to do this when your stomach isn't too full, because that can be distracting.

Now, close your eyes and take a slow, deep breath, in through your nose and out through your mouth. Be sure that on the in-breath your tongue touches the roof of your mouth. Start with a 4-second inhale...slightly hold at the top...then a 4-second exhale. You can expand this to 6 or 7 seconds as you feel comfortable. Don't completely stop the flow of air at any point; keep it continuous. Breathe from your lower abdomen, not your chest. This may feel counterintuitive at first, because in the West we've been conditioned to breathe from our chest, but your body was designed to work differently.

As you breathe, your lower abdomen should expand on the inhale and contract on the exhale. This is where your **Lower Dantien** or **Sacral Chakra**, the center of your body's energy, is located. It is also where martial artists are trained to hold their breath, to avoid getting it knocked out of them. The martial arts belt ties at this point on the abdomen, helping you center your body's energy there. Doing this makes you practically impervious to abdomen or chest strikes.

The goal is to do this slow, meditative breathing for 21 breaths, then stop and relax. While you are practicing this exercise, let go of outside thoughts and focus only on the breath. If done correctly with no distractions, you should never reach the 21st breath, because you will have entered a state of meditation before that point. At this point, you will completely forget about counting. Once you realize that you have actually reached this state it will be likely that you will have forgotten what number you had reached before forgetting to count.

Don't feel bad if it doesn't happen on the first try. Keep practicing, and at some point, you will reach your personal Nirvana in the breath. Once you master this practice, you will realize that you are always only one breath away from that state! You can then use this practice during stressful situations as a calming device, to shift your heart and mind into a state of peace and calmness in the midst of the storm. This will literally transform your ability to handle stressful situations.

As you become attuned to your internal sense of gnosis, it will guide you to your next step. The whole point of meditation is to connect with your internal divine spark of the eternal flame. As you develop your practice, you will hear that small, still voice that Yeshua spoke about. Then you will understand the true power of prayer, because you will be communing with God rather than just asking for things. I promise that at this point you will see more power in your prayers than ever before. Your personal doorway to the spirit world will have been opened, and you will have taken that first glorious step toward a new reality.

I wish you the best of luck on your meditation journey, and I pray that you will be touched by the Spirit in ways you never imagined. **Christos Domini!**

Chapter-11: Re-Examine the Words of Christ

It has been said that "Spirituality" is the act of tuning into the spiritual side of life. - "***For those who have ears, let them hear...***"

Spiritual Awakening is when you actually wake up to the truth that you are one with Prime Source or God! - "***I AM in the Father and the Father is in Me...***"

Christ Consciousness is the state of being that Yeshua talked about when he said *"God's kingdom is coming, but not in a way that you will be able to see with your eyes. People will not say, 'Look, here it is!' or, 'There it is!' because **God's kingdom is within you**."*

When Yeshua was being accused of Blasphemy by the Jews for saying he was the Son of God, he responded to them with their own religious text found in **Psalm 82**:

John 10:34 - *Jesus answered them, "Is it not written in your Law, '**I have said you are "gods"**'? If he called them 'gods,' to whom the word of God came—and Scripture cannot be set aside— what about the one whom the Father set apart as his very own and sent into the world? Why then do you accuse me of blasphemy because I said, '**I AM** God's Son'?*

In this scripture Yeshua was acknowledging that we all are to be considered as "Sons of God", because we all came from Universal Consciousness, which can be substituted for the word God in this context. God is the source of the Quantum Field from which all things spring into being. This reality is nothing more than Maya…an illusion. The only thing that is **REAL** is **Consciousness**. Science will ultimately show this, and it will not be much longer now…

Yeshua spent much of his time teaching those around him about the Truth of Gnosis, which is the Right-Brain conceptualization of reality. For this aspect of consciousness does not require proof or evidence in order to believe. It just **knows Truth**:

John 8:31-32 - *So Jesus said to the Jews who believed in him, "If you continue to obey my teaching, you are truly my followers. Then **you will know the truth**, and the truth will make you free."*

Awakening and Spirituality are both part of Ascension. For when you start to awaken to your own sense of Spirituality inside yourself, the Universe will meet you right where you are and give you exactly what it is that you need in that moment. - "***Ask, and it shall be given you;*** *seek, and ye shall find; knock, and it shall be opened unto you: For every one that asketh receiveth; and he that seeketh findeth; and **to him that knocketh it shall be opened**.*"

The "**Breath of Life**" is the initial point of Awareness which you must adhere to. It is really that simple! If you can learn to focus on the one thing you must constantly do to Live, then you will begin to feel that sense of Gnosis which has been locked up inside you for so long. As you learn to take control of your Awareness and Attention, you are able to wake up to the authentic nature of your True Spirit, and you empower yourself to consciously align with higher consciousness, wisdom, and with the Divine in every moment. - "***You will seek me and find me*** *when you seek me with **all your heart**"*

The game of Life is triggering more and more people to wake up from the persistent illusion, and remember the truth of our multidimensional selves by linking with Higher Consciousness (i.e. – Christ Consciousness). In addition to Awareness, Integration is an essential part of Ascension. - "*But seek ye first the kingdom of God, and his righteousness; and **all these things shall be added unto you**.*"

It is the awakening to the realization that we are not separate, but that separation is a lie which has been told to us by our Left-Brain modality. The Truth is that there is no such thing as Separation, for everything in the Universe is connected by and to Source. Universal Consciousness is that from which ALL things exist. – "*And **He is before all**, and all things **subsist together by Him**.*"

You need to cut the cords to the past and release the pain, guilt, and grief which is weighing you down. It is time to forgive yourself, as you forgive others, for forgiveness is the doorway to the realm of God – "**Forgive us** our trespasses, **as we forgive those** who have trespassed against us..." Once you are truly able to forgive, then Life becomes a completely different experience in which you feel and know the true power of Unconditional Love!

It is up to each individual to internally awaken, shift, and ascend, so that we are able to view reality through the lens of Love. For Love is ultimately the source of ALL - "*A new command I give you: **Love one another**. As I have loved you, so you must love one another.*"

One person at a time a wave of awareness is growing around the world. The once hidden teachings of Love, Enlightenment, and Ascension are no longer concealed by mystery schools, religion, and secret societies. – *"the **mystery that was hidden** for ages and generations but is now revealed to His saints, to whom God has chosen to make known among the Gentiles the glorious riches of this mystery, which is **Christ in you** (i.e. – Christ Consciousness), the hope of glory..."*

You are God's Masterpiece (i.e. – A Piece of the Master!). So, let no one tell you that you are not good enough, for you **ARE GOOD!** Even those who have chosen darkness on their path in life will ultimately see and know Truth. For remember, one cannot truly appreciate the Light until they have been submersed in total darkness. We all are capable of doing both good and evil in the eyes of men. It is merely a choice of experience in the here and now. Once one has experienced enough pain through darkness, he will eventually also choose Light.

Intuitive Knowing goes beyond one's belief system. It is the Right-Brain awareness which is able to experience and know through Gnosis. This knowing is far greater than any type of Left-Brain understanding, for it is felt to the core of one's existence. It is beyond that which can be understood, because it is felt outside of the conscious thinking process in the **field of awareness**, from which all things emanate!

This is your birthright and your destiny! No longer does one need to practice esoteric rituals for years in order to ascend, for our entire planet is reaching the point of a new level of ascension. Ultimately, all will understand and know this path for themselves, but for those of us who are already feeling this intuitive tug of awareness, it is our destiny to push into our own internal Christ Consciousness. For when enough people on the Earth have truly awakened, then at some point the momentum created will be enough to carry all mankind fully into it as a reality!

*"There is a **consciousness** which is here to help us on this planet, but they cannot intervene until there is a large enough presence of **consciousness** on the planet asking them to intervene."* - Carl Jung…

Final Words

In my final words, I thought I would leave you with a few of Yeshua's final words…

Blessed are the poor in spirit, for theirs is the kingdom of heaven.
Blessed are those who mourn, for they will be comforted.
Blessed are the meek, for they will inherit the earth.
Blessed are those who hunger and thirst for righteousness, for they will be filled.
Blessed are the merciful, for they will be shown mercy.
Blessed are the pure in heart, for they will see God.
Blessed are the peacemakers, for they will be called children of God.
Blessed are those who are persecuted because of righteousness, for theirs is the kingdom of heaven.

Peace…

Bibliography

Abke, Aaron. *The Gospell Conspiracy*. 4DUniversity.com, 2024.

Africanus, Julius. *Chronography quoted in Origen, Contra Celsum*

Armstrong, Karen. *Buddha*. New York: Penguin Books, 2001.

Avigad, Nahman. *Discovering Jerusalem*. Nashville: Thomas Nelson, 1983.

Bar-Serapion, Mara. *Letter to His Son, in F.F. Bruce, Jesus and Christian Origins Outside the New Testament*. Grand Rapids, MI: Eerdmans Publishing, 1974.

Barber, Malcolm. *The Cathars: The Most Successful Heresy of the Middle Ages*. Manchester: Manchester University Press, 1995.

Barnstone, Willis; Meyer, Marvin. *The Gnostic Bible*. Boston: Shambhala, 2003.

Barton, John. *A History of the Bible: The Book and Its Faiths*. New York: Viking, 2019.

Biran, Avraham; Naveh, Joseph. "*An Aramaic Stele Fragment from Tel Dan*". Israel Exploration Journal 43, no. 2/3 (1993).

Boyce, Mary. *Zoroastrians: Their Religious Beliefs and Practices*. London: Routledge & Kegan Paul, 1979.

Braden, Gregg. *The Divine Matrix: Bridging Time, Space, Miracles, and Belief*. Carlsbad, CA: Hay House, 2007.

Brown, Michael L. *Jeremiah: A Commentary Based on Ancient Jewish and Christian Sources*. Peabody, MA: Hendrickson Publishers, 2010.

Campbell, Gordon. *Bible: The Story of the King James Version, 1611-2011.* Oxford: Oxford University Press, 2010

Campbell, Joseph. *The Power of Myth.* New York: Doubleday, 1988.

Cayce, Edgar. *Edgar Cayce on Atlantis.* New York: A.R.E. Press, 1968.

Cayce, Edgar. *Edgar Cayce's Egypt: Psychic Revelations on the Most Fascinating Civilization Ever Known.* New York: A.R.E. Press, 2004.

Celsus. *The True Doctrine,* quoted in Origen, *Against Celsus.*

Chapman, James. "*The World's Most Popular Books.*" ResearchGate, 2014.

Charles, R.H. ed. *The Book of Enoch.* Oxford: Clarendon Press, 1912

Cotterell, Maurice. *The Many Lives of Jesus: The Christ Revealed.* London: Piatkus, 2004.

de Landa, Diego. *Relacion de las Cosas de Yucatan, trans. William Gates.* Baltimore: The Maya Society, 1937.

Douglas-Klotz, Neil. *Prayers of the Cosmos: Meditations on the Aramaic Words of Jesus.* San Francisco: HarperOne, 1990.

Dunn, James D.G. *The New Perspective on Paul.* Grand Rapids: Eerdmans, 2005

Easwaran, Eknath. *The Bhagavad Gita: A New Translation.* Tomales, CA: Nilgiri Press, 2007.

Ehrman, Bart D. *Lost Christianities: The Battles for Scripture and the Faiths We Never Knew.* New York: Oxford University Press, 2003.

Elkins, Don; Rueckert, Carla; McCarty, Jim. *The Ra Material: An Ancient Astronaut Speaks, 1st ed.* Louisville, KY: Schiffer Publishing, 1984.

Frend, W.H.C. *Martyrdom and Persecution in the Early Church: A Study of Conflict from the Maccabees to Donatus.* New York: Oxford University Press, 1965.

Funk, Robert W. *The Acts of Jesus: What Did Jesus Really Do?* San Francisco: HarperSanFrancisco, 1998.

George, Andrew R. *The Epic of Gilgamesh: A New Translation.* London: Penguin Classics, 1999.

González, Justo L. *The Story of Christianity, Volume 1: The Early Church to the Dawn of the Reformation.* San Francisco: HarperOne, 2010.

Hancock, Graham. *Heaven's Mirror: Quest for the Lost Civilization.* London: Michael Joseph, 1998

Hanh, Thich Nhat. *The Heart of the Buddha's Teaching: Transforming Suffering into Peace, Joy, and Liberation.* New York: Broadway Books, 1998.

Harner, Michael. *The Way of the Shaman.* San Francisco: Harper & Row, 1980

HeartMath Institute Research Staff. *Heart Intelligence: Connecting with the Intuitive Guidance of the Heart.* Boulder Creek, CA: Waterfront Press, 2016.

Hoffmeier, James K. *Israel in Egypt: The Evidence for the Authenticity of the Exodus Tradition.* Oxford: Oxford University Press, 1997.

Jacobsen, Thorkild. *The Harps That Once...: Sumerian Poetry in Translation.* New Haven, CT: Yale University Press, 1987.

Josephus, Flavius. *The Antiquities of the Jews, Book 18*. Penguin Classics, 1973.

Kaplan, Aryeh. *Meditation and Kabbalah.* York Beach, ME: Weiser Books, 1982.

Keener, Craig S. *The Gospel of Matthew: A Socio-Rhetorical Commentary.* Grand Rapids: Eerdmans, 2009.

King, Karen L. *The Gospel of Mary of Magdala: Jesus and the First Woman Apostle.* Santa Rosa, CA: Polebridge Press, 2003.

Kovacs, Betty J. *Merchants of Light: The Consciousness That Is Changing the World.* Bloomington, IN: The Kamlak Center, 2019.

Kovacs, Betty J. *The Miracle of Death: There Is Nothing But Life.* Bloomington, IN: Trafford Publishing, 2003.

Kuhrt, Amélie. *The Persian Empire: A Corpus of Sources from the Achaemenid Period.* London: Routledge, 2007.

Jung, Carl G. *The Gnostic Jung and Other Essays on Psychology and Religion.* Princeton: Princeton University Press, 2002.

Lemaire, André. "*The Mesha Stele and the Omri Dynasty,*". Biblical Archaeology Review 20, no. 3 (1994).

Lewis, C.S. *The Great Divorce.* New York: Macmillan, 1946.

Lucian of Samosata. *The Death of Peregrine.* Clarendon Press, 1905

Mazar, Eilat. *The Palace of King David: Excavations at the Summit of the City of David.* Jerusalem: Shoham Academic Research and Publication, 2009.

McCraty, Rollin. *Science of the Heart: Exploring the Role of the Heart in Human Performance.* Boulder Creek, CA: HeartMath Institute, 2015

McCraty, Rollin. *The Energetic Heart: Bioelectromagnetic Interactions Within and Between People.* Boulder Creek, CA: HeartMath Institute, 2015.

Montefiore, Simon Sebag. *Jerusalem: The Biography.* New York: Knopf, 2011.

Neusner, Jacob. *The theology of Talmud.* University of Chicago Press, 1999

Origen. *Against Celsus, Book 2.* Cambridge University Press, 1980.

Pagels, Elaine. *The Gnostic Gospels.* New York: Vintage Books, 1979.

Pearsall, Paul. *The Heart's Code: Tapping the Wisdom and Power of Our Heart Energy.* New York: Broadway Books, 1998.

Pelikan, Jaroslav. *The Christian Tradition: A History of the Development of Doctrine, Volume 1: The Emergence of the Catholic Tradition (100-600).* Chicago: University of Chicago Press, 1971.

Pliny the Younger. *Letters, Book 10.* Penguin Classics, 2003.

Porges, Stephen W. *The Polyvagal Theory: Neurophysiological Foundations of Emotions, Attachment, Communication, and Self-Regulation.* New York: W.W. Norton & Company, 2011

Reich, Ronny; Shukron, Eli. *"The Discovery of the Siloam Pool in Jerusalem".* Biblical Archaeology Review 31, no. 5 (2005)

Riley-Smith, Jonathan. *The Crusades: A History.* New Haven: Yale University Press, 2005.

Robinson, James M. ed. *The Nag Hammadi Library*. San Francisco: Harper & Row, 1988.

Rumi, Jalaluddin. *The Essential Rumi*. San Francisco: HarperOne, 1995.

Schaff, Philip. *History of the Christian Church, Volume III: Nicene and Post-Nicene Christianity*. Grand Rapids, MI: Eerdmans, 1910.

Strassman, Rick. *DMT: The Spirit Molecule*. Rochester, VT: Park Street Press, 2001.

Suetonius, *The Lives of the Caesars: The Life of Claudius*. Penguin Classics, 2007.

Tacitus, Cornelius. *Annals*. 15.44

Taylor, Jill Bolte. *My Stroke of Insight: A Brain Scientist's Personal Journey*. New York: Viking, 2008.

Torczyner, Harry. *The Lachish Letters*. Oxford: Oxford University Press, 1938.

Tzu, Lao. *Tao Te Ching*. New York: Harper & Row, 1988.

Van Auken, John; Little, Lora. *Edgar Cayce's Tales of Ancient Egypt*. Virginia Beach: A.R.E. Press, 2000.

Vermes, Geza. *The Complete Dead Sea Scrolls in English*. London: Penguin Books, 2004.

Wright, N.T. *Jesus and the Victory of God*. Minneapolis: Fortress Press, 1996.

Wright, N.T. *The Resurrection of the Son of God*. Minneapolis: Fortress Press, 2003.

Zaehner, R.C. *The Bhagavad Gita: With the Commentary of Sankara*. Oxford: Oxford University Press, 1986.

www.ingramcontent.com/pod-product-compliance
Lightning Source LLC
Chambersburg PA
CBHW060829050426
42453CB00008B/634